Left Winger

A Conservative's Guide to Enlightenment

by BALON B. BRADLEY

Left Winger

Cover design by Kim Schlossberg Designs

Table of Contents

Prologue

Those of you who purchased this book because you thought that it would be a tell-all tale from some hockey star have been tricked. You probably looked at the cover and then bought the book. I have never played ice hockey, but I love to watch the game and talk about it.

Anyway, I thank you for reading this far, and I hope that despite your initial disappointment, you will think you got your money's worth.

One of the main reasons that I wrote this book is because I think that most people are really Left Wingers or at least left of center and not Right Wingers. I do not know how it happened that so many people have come to believe that being a Left Winger is bad and being a Right Winger is virtuous. I hope that in my small way, I can set the record straight. As I like to say, "Left is right, and right is wrong most of the time."

After you read over a few chapters, you folks that think you are Right Wingers may realize that you are really Left Wingers at heart. (Maybe)

It would probably be a good idea for me to try to define what I think a Left Winger is. Since Left Wingers are unique in their individual views, as I guess Right Wingers are also; Left

Wingers will not fall into a single definition. However, I will give it my best shot to define what I think a Left Winger is.

A Left Winger is someone who believes that this is the best time in the history of the world to live. Left Wingers do not yearn for the "good old days." We think that the good old days are now and will be on into the future. You will not hear a Left Winger whine about "how the country is going to hell in a hand basket," unless you talk to one just after a losing election. Left Wingers are *optimistic about the present and the future*. We think that the world is a better place due in large part to the contributions of past Left Wingers and will be a better place to live in the future due to the contributions of Left Wingers today and tomorrow.

Left Wingers do not believe that mankind is totally depraved. With all due respect to my Calvinist friends, we just do not believe that everyone is completely bad through and through. I think that we believe that everyone suffers from human frailty of character, intellect, action, and faith, but that everybody has God-given talents, as well.

Left Wingers believe in the Constitution of the United States of America. We believe that our forefathers were Left Wingers who were trying their best to establish a nation that would give people freedoms that were unavailable to people in other countries around the globe. I want to add right here that despite the greatness of these men who were our forefathers, they certainly were wrong about some aspects of our government and society; for example: slavery, racial equity, Native American and women's rights. That is a whole lot to be wrong about, but they still created this precious Constitution and the Bill of Rights.

Left Wingers believe that societal change is inevitable. Society evolves. Evolution is a struggle, but in this great country, things always get better, not worse.

We believe that power can and does corrupt, but it does not have to corrupt all the time. We believe that the American Government is really people and not some huge evil giant. We believe in the vote. We have confidence in the system even when the Right Wingers prevail in elections. We look at our election losses as a temporary setback.

If any Right Wingers are still reading the book, you need to sit down right now before you read the next paragraph.

We believe that the American Government should be and is good. We think that public service is a great endeavor, and people should celebrate its greatness. We honor our politicians. We do not denigrate them (except for the really extreme Right Wingers). We have enormous respect for those who work as bureaucrats in our government. Those are the people who make our country work.

We believe that our elected officials must be accountable for the best interests of our country. We do not believe that people seek public office just to get rich.

We think that Right Wingers are wrong when they automatically think that every aspect of the private sector is better, more efficient, and more honest than the government. I would just ask who would you rather have fighting next to you: a mercenary or a citizen soldier.

We really believe in public education. We believe that the public education of our children is one of the highest priorities that we have. We do not have a grudge against private education;

we just think that every person should be entitled (yes entitled) to an excellent public education. Public education is the future of our country. We bristle when we hear Right Wingers denigrate our public education system.

Left Wingers believe that what is best for the working person is almost always best for our country. I will talk about that later in the book, but the engine that drives this great country forward is the working middle class. We believe that the middle class should be and is the heart of this country. We believe that Right Wingers believe that the wealthy and the very upper tip of the middle class are the heart of the country. This is a big difference between the Left and the Right. Left Wingers believe to their core that the government should not give the wealthy any legal advantage over working people. We believe that being wealthy is enough of an advantage.

Lastly, we believe that there are good people on both sides of the ice. We are amazed that some Right Wingers think that their team is the only side of virtue, when the goodness and badness of both sides is so obviously equal.

That is my best working definition of a Left Winger.

The book will reveal some of my thoughts about a variety of hot button issues in the Lefty v. Righty debate.

I hope you enjoy it.

Let's keep reading!

Tell your friends to buy a copy. It is pretty cheap.

~ Balon

Religion, Family Values and Abortion

This must seem like a crazy chapter combination, and I guess it is. This is my first book and you will appreciate that occasionally it is hard for me to figure what ought to go where. I am going to take my best swing, and here it is. As Babe Ruth once said, "Don't let the fear of striking out hold you back." I think that is great advice. This is the best I could do and that is that.

Your friendly author was born in Arkansas in 1953, but his parents were Texans and frankly, were horrified that their fine boy might be known as an "Arkie" his whole life. Anyway, like lots of Americans at the time, my dad was in the military and my mom was a housewife. Both my parents were Christians: my mother an active Methodist and my father a semi-active Baptist. Anyway, they got me to Texas as fast as they could.

I wasn't old enough to have any say as to where I was born, what denomination I was going to be, or what my political inclination would be. I just grew up and absorbed my family values.

I was six years old when my father was killed in an industrial accident. My father was a chemist and owned a chemical plant that exploded. That was a pivotal point in my life, although I certainly was not able to grasp it at the time.

That tragedy forced my mother to rethink her life and try to figure out what she was going to do with two young boys. I was six and my brother was two. Mother was no regular individual. My dad had a Ph. D. in Chemistry from The University of Texas, and my mother figured that getting a Ph. D. would allow her to get a better job than she could get without it. So mother worked full time, reared two boys, and got her Masters Degree and Ph.D. in Science Education from the same University of Texas.

While mother was going to school, raising my brother and me, and working, she was always active in our small Methodist Church in Austin, Texas. Mother taught children, helped run the Sunday School Program, sang in the choir, and was not shy about telling "Who needed what and when."

Mother wanted me to know that Methodists were more liberal than Baptists. My paternal grandmother was a Baptist, and I certainly learned a lot from her as well. Most of the family was Methodist and almost everyone was a Democrat. Being a Democrat in Texas in the 50's and 60's was no big deal, since everyone in Texas, just about, was a Democrat back then. Most of my friends are Baptists, and I am certainly not trying to pick a fight with them (they hold grudges like "the dickens"). Almost every one of them would be proud to claim that Baptists are more conservative than Methodists.

In the 1950's, being a Methodist in Texas did not necessarily make you a Lefty; it just was an indication that you leaned more toward the left than, say, a Baptist.

I do not remember the exact date, but the Methodist Church united and became the United Methodist Church. I will never forget the first Sunday after the Methodist Church united.

What I did not really appreciate was the reason that the church "United." Frankly, I am not completely certain now, but I do know that it had something to do with the unification of the church after the denomination split up during the Civil War. Anyway, we went to church as we did every Sunday, and to my surprise, only about half the normal crowd was there that day. When I asked my mother what was happening, she replied that a lot of the folks were afraid that we would be "overrun with negroes." I might add that "negro" was the word that we used to describe people of African American descent at that time. Others were using less sensitive language to describe African Americans then. I guess that not everyone was as liberal in our little church as we were.

After mother earned her Ph. D., she accepted a teaching position at McMurry College in Abilene, Texas. I might add that McMurry was and is a Methodist College. It is now McMurry University. I was 14 years old. I had lived in Austin, which is or at least was a pretty liberal place (except for maybe race relations). It was the home of The University of Texas Longhorns, hippies, nudists, free thinkers, dope addicts, liberals, intellectuals, and a heck of a lot of fine people. I would soon realize how different an environment I was going to experience in Abilene, Texas.

When we lived in Austin, almost all of my mother's friends were like-minded people, and I pretty much thought that everybody thought like my mother did. At that time, I was only really learning to think and begin my own version of liberal thinking. (Some of my friends still think that I have just now started to learn to think on my own.)

In Abilene, we joined the Methodist Church that was right across the street from McMurry College. I have to admit, I was very proud of my mother even though I have come to learn that "pride is considered a sin."

Now, I do not want anybody to think that I have any axe to grind with any of the good folks in Abilene; I do not. In fact, if there were a better place to grow up in middle class America, I would not believe it. Abilene was a great place to grow up and live.

It is not my intention to talk about religion just in Abilene, although I would bet there is more religion in Abilene per capita than anywhere else in the world, with the possible exception of the Vatican.

My kind of religion is that "Old Time Religion." What does that mean to me? It means Bible reading, loud hymn singing, and regular church attendance. As a child, I went to church twice on Sunday and at least one more evening. I bet a lot of you did also.

This is the point in this chapter where I go from talking to meddling. Everybody knows if you have good sense you do not talk about religion or politics. I plan on talking about both: religion first.

Like a heck of a lot of Left Wingers, I strongly believe that Jesus is the Messiah, the Christ, the Son of God, God Incarnate, the Beginning (Middle) and the End and part of the Holy Trinity. As I began to study a little more in my Bible, I learned that the words Messiah and Christ both meant the same thing: the Anointed One. I had always thought until I was about 50 years old that those words would literally mean the Son of God. I am now a Presbyterian and the more I study, the more fascinated I am with the Word of God.

I am so thankful that I finally read the Bible from start to finish. It has given me insight that I otherwise would never have. I have to admit that there were parts in the Old Testament that were hard to get through, but the knowledge and spiritual enlightenment was really worth it. If you have not read the entire Bible, I suggest that you do so immediately after reading this book.

I believe in the power of prayer. If you take nothing else from this book; take this: prayer is powerful and prayer works. If more people, both Lefties and Righties, prayed, our world would be a much, much better place. I swear I believe this.

I think the biggest difference in Christian religion between the Left Wingers and the Right Wingers is the way they interpret the Bible. That seems like a patently obvious and dull remark, except it goes to the heart of the differences. In my opinion, Left Wingers interpret the Bible and are not afraid to admit it. Right Wingers claim to believe in the Bible word for word, and they claim they do not interpret the Bible because it is God's Word; it is straight forward and not open to interpretation. I am no Biblical scholar, but I know everybody interprets the Bible. That is why we have different denominations, some of which are more liberal and some are more conservative. My maternal grandmother was a fine Christian woman. At her funeral, my brilliant and liberal Uncle David spoke of her great faith. He stated that she believed the Bible. It did not matter what the Bible said; she believed it. It did not matter whether the Bible said the whale swallowed Jonah or Jonah swallowed the whale, she believed what the Bible said and that is that.

There are scriptures that are really hard to understand. I think that it is impossible for any mere human to understand everything that the Bible tells us. That is part of the mystery of God's greatness and supernatural nature. Since parts of the Bible are so difficult to understand, I believe all of us interpret the best that we can. Left Wingers rely on our denomination, our church, theological scholars, our preachers, our spiritual leaders, our fellow Christians, our prayer, and our own god given intellect and talents to interpret what we think is a theologically proper interpretation of the Bible.

Many Right Wingers have a different idea. Somehow they think that the way that they understand the Bible is the *only* way. They do not seem to be able to recognize that they have their particular interpretation. They, certainly not all, believe that they have the *only* interpretation. If a person disagrees with the way a Right Winger thinks what the Bible says, that means that the other person is wrong, wrong and wrong. If it is a little point like "dunking" versus "sprinkling," it is only a small theological mistake. If it is about a more serious issue, the wrong thinker is probably going to Hell. If you are not familiar with the controversy of sprinkling versus dunking, then you need to go to church a little more.

My conservative Christian friends believe that the Bible tells us that being a Christian is the *ONLY* way to get to Heaven. I have a slightly different philosophy. I think that being a Christian is the ONLY GUARANTEED, CERTAIN, FOR SURE way of going to Heaven. Before you folks think I am out of my mind, I will mention that there are references in the Old Testament of people who were not Christians going to Heaven. Another example of non-Christians going to Heaven is the transfiguration in the New Testament, where Moses and Elijah appeared with Jesus. I have always believed that they appeared from Heaven and not somewhere else. Now, if I am correct, then you go figure. If I am wrong, then you can say, "Well, that boy is a liberal."

My big break with my conservative Christian friends is **that I think God has the power to select whomever He chooses to go to Heaven.** I will stake my future with Jesus, but I am not going to tell God or you who goes to Heaven and who does not. Believe me, that is too big a job even for this big left wing boy.

Another thing that riles me up is the idea that someone is a better Christian than someone else, simply because he or she belongs to this church or that church or drinks booze or does not or does or does not do a lot of other things. Certainly, some of us live more righteous lives than others of us, but the idea that someone is a better Christian than someone else is absurd to me. Who is the judge? I think that the old epitaph that he or she was a "Good Christian or a Fine Christian" is well and good as it is meant to say that someone lived a good life and was an honest person who tried to live the life that he or she thought God had in mind. However, for some group to think that they are "better Christians" than another group seems bizarre to me. As you read this book, are you thinking, "I am a better Christian than Balon" or God forbid, "Balon is a better Christian than I am?" If you have thought in the past that someone might be a better Christian, now that you reflect upon it, hopefully, you do not really believe it anymore. I am sure that many of you have indeed read the Bible. Remember Matthew 11:19. If one were to think that drinkers are sinners, how does this verse compute?

I have a great deal of respect for the Catholic Church. I am a Protestant, but I believe that God has used and is using the Catholic Church for His Glory. All denominations have their bad apples, and certainly the Catholic Church has had its share, but it is obvious that it has been and is so important to

God's Will. Where I have been amazed is the idea that some of my conservative Christian cohorts think that Catholics are not really Christians. I am wondering who gives these people the authority to make those judgments? (Remember, who THE JUDGE is!) This was big time conservative Christian thinking when I was growing up, and you could hear it all the time from conservative pulpits. Now I hear this less and less, I think, because so many Catholics are conservative. It is too problematic for the Right Wingers to fight it out when there are those Left Wingers out there that need to be characterized as godless liberals. I suggest you go drinking with one of your Right Wing, non-Catholic, buddies and get started talking about Catholics. It will come out. It has to make you wonder; if Catholics are not Christians, who are? Are Catholics getting together and saying that Protestants are not Christians? Maybe I will go drinking with a Catholic buddy and try to pry it out of him. I doubt they feel that way.

You have to wonder about the Republicans. Although they want to talk about the "Big Tent" that their party encompasses, are there any vocal liberal theological members of the Republican Party? Are there any agnostics? Are there any atheists? What about Jews? If you really want to get a conservative Christian going, ask them about Mormons. You do not even have to take them drinking to hear them talking bad about Mormons. I do wonder how it is that there are so many conservative Mormons. When I am really on a roll, I prank my extremely conservative Christian friends with the terrible quandary they face with a Republican Mormon running against a liberal Democrat for President. I tell you it is like lighting their hair on fire it upsets them so much to think about it. Is there any doubt that the Republican Party calls itself the party of the conservative Christian? If faith in God is as important to

Republicans as they say it is, then I cannot see how they could reconcile having non "right thinking" Christians in the party. Many Republicans tell anyone who will listen that their party is the only party where God-loving Christians can possibly be found. Oh my gosh, if you are a Democrat or have some other party affiliation, you are in trouble.

That is one of the big lies that *some* of the Right Wingers in the Republican Party promulgate. These Right Wingers claim that the Republican Party is the party of Christian faith and the Democrats are the party of atheists, agnostics, liberals, egg heads, homos, minorities, special interest groups, labor unions, communists, pinkos; you name it, but no Christians. The Right Wingers motto seems to be: If it is bad theologically, or otherwise, it must be liberal. I would be embarrassed to be a member of a political party that was so full of hubris that its members believed that their party was so virtuous and the other party was full of people just waiting to go to Hell.

The problem is that there are people in this great country that actually believe that tripe. Let us look at the truth. Does anyone in his or her right mind really believe that conservative Christians are more Christian than liberal Christians? Can anyone believe that Right Wingers are not subject to the same sinful temptations that Left Wingers are? Do Right Wingers have some gift from God that makes them more virtuous than the rest of us? The answer is, of course not. Shame on you that have been duped into believing that! Who made anyone that judge? All Christians should know WHO does the judging, when the judging really counts. I am telling you one thing: it darn sure is not a Republican! I might add it is not a Democrat either. Let's face it: all of us are sinners, not just the Left Wingers. If that is too much for my Right Wing readers to digest, then

I suggest you stop reading at this point and contemplate your theology on this issue for a few hours. (Please pick the book back up after you have finished contemplating.)

I am going to make a *really big controversial point* right here. Mainline Christians believe that Jesus judges the living and the dead. What does this judging mean? It means that the one and only Jesus (the Triune God Himself) judges who is a Christian and who is not or, perhaps, who is on his team and who is not. That is not the controversial part. The controversial part is this: what do you call someone who is a Christian who takes to judging who is a Christian and who is not? In other words, what are we to think when we hear a person essentially say that he or she can make the judgment as to whom is a Christian and who is not? In essence, this person is saying that he or she is going to take this role away from Jesus and proclaim it for him or herself. Is this person assuming to oneself the rights or qualities of God? What is a definition of this activity? Here is what Dictionary.com says: *Blasphemy:* "the crime of assuming to oneself the rights or qualities of God." So what is a person who does this? Perhaps this person is a blasphemer? This is not a charge many Christian people would want to face. Who gives anyone the right to call Barack Obama a Muslim? Who has that authority? It is a shocking and blasphemous claim. Judgment belongs to Jesus not some knucklehead who thinks it is a good put down for the President. I would think twice before I made that outrageous, blasphemous and I believe, false claim!

Now, before you think I am some kind of religious zealot, I do think it is fine to say so and so is not living the kind of life that *I think* a Christian should. Or that so and so has not demonstrated the kind of life that *I would hope* that a Christian would live. This is an opinion; perhaps a dumb one, but it is an opinion. However, to say that this person or that person is not a Christian as a fact is obscene. Shame on every person who has uttered that sentence! Fortunately, the Lord forgives blasphemers!

I am still going crazy over this! Left Wingers really are more open-minded on this issue. We realize that we are sinners, and we are no better or no worse than our Right Wing brethren. I do not know whether there are any more Left Wingers in the Republican Party, but I do know there are still some Right Wingers in the Democratic Party (at least two). I also know that the Democratic Party welcomes people from all religions, and those people are not afraid to speak out about their faith. I do not know how so many theologically intolerant people can get together to vote in the same party. It boggles my mind! How can the Republicans win the Presidency or even a state-wide election with this kind of thinking?

This Left Winger is not just going to sit by and let people be tricked into thinking all Christians are conservative. They are not. As a matter of fact, I believe that there are more Left Winger Christians than Right Winger Christians! I base this belief in part because I believe that there are a lot of Left Wingers out there who have been tricked into believing they are Right Wingers. Once they see the light, there will certainly be a clear majority. I am not saying there are not plenty of Right Wing Christians. I think there are plenty of them, and I thank God for them, too.

Before I leave the issue of religion, I have to tell you that I am startled that a lot of my Righty friends do not believe that Muslims believe in the same God as we Christians do. Now, of all my friends who assert that opinion, not one of them has ever read the Koran, but they are certain in this belief. All I can say is read the Koran, or if that is too time consuming, ask a Muslim if Muslims worship the same God as the God of Abraham.

I thought that I would wade into the family values issue, which is certainly not completely interrelated with religion, but at least in my life, it is closely connected.

Once again, I am no expert on family values; I just know that neither Left Wingers nor Right Wingers have a lock on having family values to the exclusion of others. Also, all of us who are married and have raised children know how difficult it is to instill family values.

I want to first discuss basic family values and try to make a distinction between family values and religious values despite the fact that they are one in the same for many of us.

When I think of family values, I think of the characteristics that will make a person a valuable member of their family, their community, and of the society. These issues, in my opinion, are somewhat different from religious values. In other words, an atheist can raise children that can grow up and become adults who are productive and valuable members of our society. As an aside, one of the problems I have with religious people is that it is sometimes almost impossible to distinguish people of faith from atheists. It just seems to me that there should be some observable differences. Think about it. Could any of us Christians, Left Winger or Right Winger, be observed to be living a more virtuous life than a Jew, a Buddhist, a Muslim, an Atheist or anyone else? If we take out church attendance, and many Christians have already done that, what differences could we tell? What type of family values or Christian values would be glowing from our Christian countenance that would separate us from our fellow non-Christian citizens?

What are some of the characteristics that form the basis of family values?

Politeness, honesty, respect for others, knowledge of right from wrong, fairness, discipline, industriousness, respect for authority, and love of family are some of the non-religious and non-political values that make up what I call family values. This is neither a list of political values, nor economic values, nor religious values. It is just some common sense values that all people should possess.

Religious values are theological in their basis. Yes, many of us claim to adhere to the Ten Commandments, which, of course, are in the Bible, but I think of religious values as theological in their nature. Hopefully, good theology promotes good family and societal values, but they are somewhat different.

Is there a person who never violates one or more of these virtues? I doubt it. Still, despite our foibles, I believe most us Left Wingers and Right Wingers do about the same in this arena. We try to instill these virtues and others in our children, and we hope that our children grow up to be productive and valuable members of our society.

The irony to me is that lots of Right Wingers believe the propaganda that Left Wingers do not promote family values and that only Right Wingers seem to possess these values. This belief is so ridiculous that it boggles my mind. Do Right Wingers believe that Left Wingers teach their children to lie, be rude, disrespect others, break the law, spit on fairness, be lazy, and hate their family? If you listen to some Right Wingers, you would believe that they must have this belief.

Wake up folks! *Every good parent*, regardless of political or religious ideology, is doing his or her best to instill family values into their children. If you believe that either the Right or the Left is more family value oriented than the other, I suggest that you sit down (if your are not already doing so) and repeat this, "I wonder how I could have been duped into such a preposterous notion that my team is more virtuous than your team." Repeat this about ten times to yourself and then do not ever be duped again on this issue.

What are some of the biggest problems we face? I believe having children out of wedlock is certainly one of these. Children having children is a huge problem. It is not a new phenomenon, but it seems to me to be a growing one now. Why are there so many out of wedlock births by children? One of the biggest reasons, at least in my Left Wing opinion, is a breakdown of family values. Somewhere, somehow, the parents of these children having children out of wedlock were unable to instill the virtue of marriage. I could go on and on about this. Do I have a solution for this problem? One solution is that I believe that we as a society have to instill better family values in our children.

There are zillions of other problems which we must address as a society, which would dramatically be impacted if our society were to really put more effort into family values. These are just a few: helping the homeless, promoting community service, honoring our parents, honoring our children, teaching the truth about temptation, honesty in relationships, attending religious services, and learning to understand and appreciate cultural and racial diversity. The list never ends. I could write pages about the problems we face, but surely you get the drift.

I am not trying to cop out and I know that sounds corny, but I believe it. We need to encourage and reeducate our society on the basics of family values. If we were able to reteach/instill family value, then this problem and many, many, more problems would improve. I do not think that this is a Left Winger or Right Winger opinion; it just seems like the truth to me.

If you still think that one side is more virtuous than the other side, then just look at your elected officials. Look at the Left Wingers and look at the Right Wingers. Check who has been divorced, who is rude, who flaunts disrespect of those who disagree with him or her, and you will see a pretty clear picture that we are all in the same boat when it comes to family values.

As I said earlier, family values are not always related to religion; however, I do believe that if we as a society honored our parents and our parents honored their children, then we would be so much to the better it would be mind boggling.

If I have not left well enough alone, I am going to really set some of you off now. This is a warning. Here is where I am going to wade into abortion. That sentence alone may indicate that I am trying to antagonize everybody, but I am not. I am just trying to explain to my Right Wing Christian friends that this is not a theological issue *per se*. It certainly has theological overtones, but I do not believe that it is primarily theological in nature.

Well, what is abortion if it is not just a theological issue? It is a medical procedure. Some people think it is murder. Some people think it is birth control. Most everyone thinks it is somewhere in the middle. What gets my goat is the naïve or arrogant position many otherwise well-meaning Christians take on this issue. It goes like this: "I am a Christian. I have

Christian values. I live a Christian life. I have Christian beliefs. I am against abortion. Abortion is unchristian. I do not believe anyone can believe in abortion and be a Christian." The last two sentences are the ones that get my Left Wing goat.

Let's talk about what is an anti-abortion or right to life position. On the one side, there are people who believe that the medical procedure of an abortion should never occur. It should be illegal and punishable with time in prison. It should not matter what extenuating circumstances exist; no abortion ever. While I do not agree with this opinion, I understand the logic behind it. It makes sense to me. These people are against abortions, period. This is a true anti-abortion position.

The people who have the Right to Life position are a much harder group to understand. It is a great slogan. I mean who is not for the right to life? There are some in this group who are really anti-abortion, but there are a lot of others, *I think the majority*, who are not so much anti-abortion in their views but more kinda anti-abortion. This group touts its anti-abortion agenda, but when it gets down to the lick log, many in this group have exceptions to the no abortion rule. The three most notable exceptions are that abortions are acceptable in the case of rape, incest, and to save the life of the mother. The politics and emotion of the abortion issue are hard. I am not trying to make light of that, and I am not trying to make fun of anyone's beliefs. What I am doing is pointing out what I consider to be some difficult issues for me to understand on the Right to Life side.

If a person believes in these exceptions to the real anti-abortion stance, how can they claim to be against abortion? If the preservation of precious life is the main thrust of the anti-abortion movement, then I do not get it. Whose life is more valuable:

the mother's or the baby conceived by rape or incest? I mean, if the preservation of life is the aim, then it seems hard to justify the rationale in the qualitative decision that an adult mother's life is more important than a baby's life, if having the baby would threaten the mother's life. But that would not seem to support the idea that life is precious and must be saved from an abortion.

This becomes even more difficult to embrace if the precious baby can be aborted because of its conception either through rape or incest. I am wholeheartedly against rape and incest; yet I do not understand the thinking that people who consider themselves to be Right to Life would carve out these exceptions.

The real rub is that some, frankly I do not know the percentage, consider the Right to Life position with these exceptions to be THE Christian view. They either overtly or implicitly believe that anyone who would disagree is not sharing a Christian belief or principal and therefore, probably is not a Christian at all, or if that person is for abortion, certainly not a "good Christian" (whoever that might be).

I have searched the Bible, and I have not found any scripture that mentions abortion. I do not believe that either side, Pro-Life or Pro-Choice, is Biblically supported. I am open minded and if such scripture exists, I will rewrite this chapter.

So what about the Pro-Choice side? Some people believe that abortion should be legal from conception to partial birth. Others believe that an abortion should only be legal during the period of time before the fetus is viable outside the womb. Others think that the government should not make abortion illegal. I think all Pro-Choice people believe that the decision is ultimately the woman's. In other words, the Pro-Choice side is not advocating that everyone go out and get an abortion; they are advocating the position that the government should not take that choice away from women by criminalizing abortion.

So what do I think? Abortion is a very emotional issue. I do not believe that it is either a Left Wing or a Right Wing issue. There are plenty of conservatives who are Pro-Choice. There are plenty of liberals who are against abortions being legal across the board. There are even some liberals who are against abortion under any circumstances. I, also, do not believe that abortion is a theological issue. There are Christians (and other types of believers) who are for the legalization of abortions. There are Christians (and other types of believers) who are anti-abortion under any situation. And, of course, there are Christians (and other believers) who are against abortion in some circumstances but not in others.

Do you think I am trying to be coy or chicken about stating my views on this issue? It should not be a surprise. I am a Christian who believes that abortion should be legal. I am not saying a person must have one, but I am saying that the government should not prohibit most abortions in this country. I am against partial-birth abortion.

Perhaps, abortion is more about family values than it is about politics.

Marriage is a bedrock principal of family values. Choosing the right spouse is not only super important, but it is frequently poorly executed. Unfortunately, the criteria that so many people (mainly young ones) use is corrupt. The biggest mistake many people make is thinking that good looks makes for good mates. I have a female friend who told me that when she was in college she had the worst judgment in boyfriends ever. She is now a very attractive and successful wife, mother, and attorney. However, when she was younger, she said if a young man was good enough looking and asked her on a date, she would not have cared if he was an axe murderer. That is how important looks were to her at that time. Fortunately for her, no axe murderers asked her out and finally she came to her senses and figured out that good looks is not the most important trait to look for in a spouse.

I certainly do not have anything against you good looking people out there, but I just want you and everybody else to know that looks should be only one (and a small one at that) trait to look for when choosing a spouse.

The person you choose to marry will have a tremendous effect on the rest of your life, the lives of your children, and the lives of those around you. Pay attention here. Choose wisely. Your choice will affect what types of values you will instill in your children and grandchildren. Do not pick a person just because they have a pretty face or a hot body. If that is your criteria, look out, you are in for trouble.

Who should you choose? How should you do it? Is there a guarantee that you will pick the right one? No, of course not. I will only say that you should try to pick someone that has a similar faith, a similar intellect, a similar set of values, a similar set of goals, and is a kind person who loves you as much as you love him or her. I am a liberal, so I think sex is important, too. Then you have to work hard to keep it together. You can be successful.

"When I was a child, I talked like a child, I thought like a child, I reasoned like a child. When I became a man, I put the ways of childhood behind me." (1 Corinthians 13:11). I can say that I adhered to the first sentence of this scripture. I waffle on the latter.

I have been in the same Bible Study since 1992. I have learned more about the Bible in that class than in every other theological endeavor I have experienced combined. It is an awesome group of very diverse guys working together to study and learn about the Bible. The formula for the great success is pretty simple. Find a super guy who has a strong theological passion to lead the group. Get a bunch of smart guys with very different backgrounds who respect each other's opinions and rotate the discussion leader every week.

Anyway, as I mentioned, I have spent a lot of time in my life at one church or another. I went to Vacation Bible School as a child and have been going to church ever since. I am now appreciating that the lessons I learned as a child are still very important to me now, although I see things very differently.

I will discuss this issue in a different chapter, but I will toss it out now. When I was a child, I learned that David (King David) was a man after God's own heart. I knew he slew Goliath with a sling and a stone. I knew that he was a great king who united the Kingdom of Israel. And I knew that he was the root of the family tree of Jesus.

As I got a little older, I learned that David could sing and dance. (For my Baptist friends, I did not make up that dancing, it is in the Bible). I learned he was a great warrior, and eventually, I learned that he somehow got mixed up with a gal named Bathsheba.

As we studied the Books of Samuel, I learned a whole lot more about David. This will be my interpretation, so do not blame every Left Winger, just me. David was a viscous killer. He lied. He essentially murdered Uriah so he could take Bathsheba after he had an adulterous relationship with her. He was a polygamist, and he had numerous concubines. (To some, this would make him a serial fornicator.) The list of his sinfulness goes on. Rather poor family values, I would think, how about you?

As we discussed David's life, it seemed that our group accepted all of the aforementioned sinfulness as "it is what it is." But when we started discussing I Samuel 20:41, things got a little testy. "After the boy had gone, David got up from the south side of the stone and bowed down before Jonathan three times, with his face to the ground. Then they kissed each other and wept together—but David wept the most." I suggested that David might have had a homosexual tendency here. This was not well received. I simply said, "It says what it says."

The point is that even in my enlightened group of Bible studiers, one seems to cross the proverbial line when we talk about homosexuality.

We will discuss why I think religious people are so anti-homosexual later. I just wanted you to start thinking about the issue.

Well, smarter people than I could write a lot more about religion, family values and abortion. Maybe smarter people would have better sense than to do it! I only want to leave you with this thought: these are very important issues. Neither Left Wingers nor Right Wingers have a right to claim that their opinion is the definitive opinion on these. If you think that your side is the bastion of this sort of virtue, you really do not have a very clear picture of what is going on in America or anywhere else.

Economics

In this book, when I talk about economics, I really want to focus on the relationship between the federal government and private enterprise.

The first subject is really easy to cover. The government should not consistently spend more than it takes in taxes. Why is that so hard to understand?

One of the misconceptions that almost all Right Wingers have is that Left Wingers just want the government to spend money and spend money and spend money without any regard for the federal budget. That, my friends, is not what Left Wingers want at all. We want responsible spending. We want our Congress to prioritize the budget in a way that really benefits the greatest good and not the pockets of one group or another. What we want is for the government to spend money on programs that are necessary and not frivolous. We bristle that Right Wingers think that Left Wingers only elect people that will provide welfare to anyone who would rather sit home, watch TV, drink booze, and eat Bon Bons than get a job and work. For those of you Right Wingers who really think that, you are in need of some therapy. Someone has brainwashed you.

Let us remember that under President Clinton, we had a budget surplus. Do I have to remind everyone that under the past three Republican Presidents we have experienced nothing but big deficit spending. Sergeant Friday used to say, "Just the Facts, Ma'am," and the facts are that Left Wingers are no bigger spenders than Right Wingers. One can quickly and accurately point out that under President Obama, the deficit has soared. I own that. The difference between most Lefties and most Righties is how to go about reducing the deficit. I believe that in the present political world Left Wingers are actually more fiscally responsible than their buddies, the Right Wingers. Why is this? Left Wingers consider the possibility that some-times taxes must be increased and that spending cuts may not be enough to get it done.

Left Wingers are for spending which helps the working people in America. Left Wingers also are sophisticated and caring enough to understand that there are lots of folks that for one reason or another cannot hold down a job, and they need public assistance. Where we draw the line at who can and who cannot hold down a job may be a big issue for debate, but there are certainly a fair number of people in this country who need welfare.

So, on what should the government spend money? There is a long list of vitally important expenditures that the government must support. Everyone would agree that we need a strong and efficient military, which is outfitted with the best equipment and weaponry that is available. We need to spend money on science and technology. (However, apparently some Right Wingers in Texas do not agree with this.) Does anyone think that our space program has not benefited us? Is there an amount of money which would not be well spent on the science and technology of alternative fuel resources? The list goes on and on. This issue is what is a prudent balance of equities? Therein is the real issue. Darn near every hard shell Right Winger really wants the government to spend money; just on the projects that they claim worthy. I guess we are all the same. The only difference is that Left Wingers are more straightforward in their desire to engage in a meaningful discussion in that we acknowledge the need for governmental expenditures. In some ways, this is like the old story about the liquor store, the Presbyterian and the Baptist. Everyone goes to the liquor store; it is just that the Baptists will not acknowledge each other, and the Presbyterians will.

I really do not think (with the exception of welfare issues) that Left Wingers and Right Wingers differ on what the government should spend money. The issue is how much and who should benefit from government spending.

Since I started writing this book, another issue has arisen: "The Taxpayer Protection Pledge." The majority of Republicans in Congress have signed it. What did they sign? Here it is:

"The signer promises to:

ONE, oppose any and all efforts to increase the marginal income tax rates for individuals and/or businesses; and

TWO, oppose any net reduction or elimination of deductions and credits, unless matched dollar for dollar by further reducing tax rates."

This sounds sooo good. How could any patriotic taxpaying American not sign this? Unfortunately, it is a Right Winger trick! Do not be fooled. It does not make sense. In fact, it poses a real threat to Americans. The heck you say, Left Winger! The heck I say.

If a person signs a pledge, what does that mean? A pledge is a solemn promise. It is something that people can rely on as the truth. A pledge should not be broken. If a person violates a pledge, that person is a pledge breaker or a prevaricator! Therefore, these elected officials have pledged not to raise income taxes. Period. Never. Not for any reason. Still sounds good to you, doesn't it? Is it implicit that if one of these individuals were to vote to raise taxes FOR ANY REASON, that person would be breaking his or her pledge, which would make him or her a pledge breaker and unworthy of office?

Here is the problem with this pledge. I think these elected officials made the pledge either because they thought it sounded so sensible, in which case, I would question their wisdom, or because they thought it would get them elected. You can hear them touting their pledge, "As long as I am your elected official, I will never raise your taxes, ever, harrumph!" Their constituents go wild and run to the election booth and elect this pledger.

Now the pledger is in office.

God forbid that we have a natural disaster of a huge magnitude, which must be managed and paid for by the federal government. Let's assume that the cost of restoration is trillions of dollars. Do these pledgers just spend us further into debt? I suppose so, since they have made the pledge. Certainly, they would not break their word because these elected representatives pledged not to raise taxes.

What if we are really forced into a full blown war? I pray that is not the case, but war costs money. These pledgers would either have to make some kind of high-falutin speech where he or she would say, "I would never raise taxes, except for now," or I suppose he or she could say, "My fellow constituents, I will not break my pledge, and I resign," or I guess he or she would just vote to spend whatever it took and let the deficit explode.

We constantly hear that our corporate tax rate is too high and that it puts American businesses at a world-wide disadvantage because our corporate taxes are too high. We Left Wingers want to be able to compete and win on a world-wide basis, and I think my Right Winger friends do, also. The kicker here is that we have large corporations right here in the good old USA not paying a dime in corporate taxes while others are paying at this high corporate tax rate. What has to happen? Either we eliminate the corporate tax all together, continue the current system that everyone seems to think is bad, or we have to make a fair corporate tax system that allows our American businesses the ability to compete on a world-wide basis.

Is it realistic that we eliminate the corporate tax? I do not think so. Do we leave our unfair and perhaps corrupt system in place? Do we institute a fair and reasonable corporate tax?

What can the pledgers do? They either have to lobby for the elimination of the corporate tax all together, or they have to keep the current unfair and corrupt system. The first option is not going to happen. It is a fairy tale.

Why do the pledgers then have to keep the unfair and corrupt corporate tax system which everyone liberal and conservative does not like? They must stay with the unfair and corrupt corporate tax system because they will have to RAISE taxes on some businesses and corporations if a uniform and fair system were implemented.

In essence, these pledgers are stuck. They must keep the unfair and corrupt corporate tax system we have to keep from raising corporate taxes on *any* corporations. Now let us listen to the pledgers as they address their now more wary and alert constituents, "Vote for me! I support an unfair and corrupt corporate tax system! I want you voters to know that I want to keep our current uncompetitive corporate tax system in place that keeps our businesses and corporations from competing on a world-wide basis!" That does not seem quite as catchy, does it? However, that is exactly the mess that these pledgers have gotten themselves, our Congress, and our citizens into.

What about all you flat taxers out there? Can the pledgers reasonably support a flat tax? Heck no, they cannot. It would raise the taxes on some people. It would raise the real tax rate on the very people that these pledgers worship, which is the richest of the rich in our country, and it would raise taxes on the poorest Americans, also. I doubt that they worry about the poor, at all, except that a pledge not to raise taxes is a pledge.

What should we as enlightened voters do with these pledgers? I think the best option is to vote them out of office as fast as possible and elect representatives who are not just trying to trick their constituents but trying to run our government in the best and most efficient way that they can. We do not need a bunch of pledgers, period. Think about it. This is not a Left Winger versus Right Winger issue. It is an issue about truth and facing difficult decisions and fairness and showing courage. None of these qualities seem to be very important to those who have signed the pledge.

We all know that the issue of the government's role in the economy is one where many Left Wingers and Right Wingers have real philosophical differences. These are frequently discussed in a civil manner and frequently not!

Let us cut to the chase. Is the United States of America a non-socialist country? All of my Right Winger friends puff up when this issue comes up and snarl that they would rather be dead than red, and they despise all the pinko socialist countries all over the world with the exception of Great Britain. They swear that the government has no business in business and that is that.

That is a problem with Right Winger thinking because the real answer is not so straight forward. The good old USA is a hybrid economy with a working blend of socialism and free enterprise. The heck you say? Yep, the heck I say. We are not nearly as socialistic as most countries, but I think that we might look at what our government does before we brag of our non pinko heritage.

So that my Right Wing friends or readers (if any are still left) will continue to read, let us not call our country or at least part of it "American Socialism"; let us call it something more manly like the United States Armed Forces. That is catchy, don't you think? How many of you out there in Right Wing land would rather have a mercenary group of fighters supported exclusively by some corporation rather than our armed forces, which are supported by American taxpayers? I think I can answer that question. There are not any of you that believe that! Yet, our armed forces have always provided the overwhelming number of troops in combat and peace, and they have always been supported by good old taxes. That was too easy.

Is Social Security something that Left Wingers want to preserve? Yes, sir, it is! How many Right Wingers want to step up and say that Social Security should be eliminated because it is socialism? Whether one believes that the government should have a program like Social Security is an interesting discussion for a civics class, but does anyone really think it should be eliminated because it is socialism? If you Right Wingers think Social Security should be eliminated, please pressure your elected representatives to enact legislation to repeal it. That will just about guarantee the election of Left Wingers to most every elected seat in Congress. You will have done more for the cause of liberalism than a million Left Winger writers could ever do. (You know it, too). I might add that the overwhelming majority of Americans, Lefties and Righties, NEED Social Security to have a safe and healthy retirement.

It is interesting to me that during stock market boom years, some Right Wingers want to privatize Social Security because they theorize that they can invest their tax dollars better than the government can. These proponents are strangely quiet during bad stock market years. As we have had a declining market, I am not hearing the call for privatization of the Social Security system very much anymore.

The idea of privatization Social Security is one of the worst ideas ever. What would happen when millions of people invested their lifetime Social Security proceeds, which they cashed in from the government and then lost all or most of the money in a disastrous market? Who would be called upon to save these Americans? You got it, the federal government. Privatization of Social Security will not work. In fact, it would lead to more government spending to bail out all the people who lost their money in the market. Does one have to be a Left Winger to see this? No, you just have to have some sense.

I think that I am on a little bit of a roll here. What do Right Wingers think about Medicare? They might think it is socialism. How many of them want to get the Republican Party revved up about eliminating Medicare? Is it a good program for our country? Has Medicare ruined our way of life? Has it hurt the group that it is intended to help? Are doctors that accept Medicare living in cardboard houses? I do not think so. How many of you Right Wingers really think that you get a better deal buying health insurance than you will receive from Medicare benefits? Is there one Right Winger in America over 65 that believes that? Is Medicare perfect? No, everyone agrees that Medicare needs constant evolutionary improvement. It amazes me that Right Wing pundits get on television and rant about Medicare. The fact that their audience approves of these rants amazes me even more!

Here are two programs that are part of the fabric of our way of life: Social Security and Medicare. Let's take a head count. How many Left Wingers think these two programs are vital to the well being of our country and need to be safeguarded and continued forever? I would say 100% feel this way. These Left Wingers will get out and vote, too. By the way, a lot of Right Wingers change their minds about this type of socialism when they get to be 65. They still hate socialism for everybody else, but for them, it is working fine, thank you.

If Right Wingers really hate socialism or government entitlement programs, then let them get behind the Republican Party and do all they can to push that agenda. I've got a secret: It's not gonna happen. Those Republican politicians are nobody's fools; they know that a certain amount of socialism goes a long way at the voting booth, and although they claim they hate it, they really support it. They are not very honest about it.

The list just goes on and on. Are we hypocrites, one and all? Maybe we are. How much of this can we bear to read?

Should the government bail out some big companies when they go broke? Most Left Wingers think that it should. Why do Left Wingers think that? They believe that the benefit of helping a big company, which employs thousands of working people, is a vital asset to the communities where these people live. Also, some industries and the companies within that industry are essential to the national well being. This is an ironic situation, because in many cases, the people who benefit most from a government bail out are rich Right Wingers who own tons of stock or are in management positions and have let the company decline under their watch. Left Wingers are willing to help one and all. Heck, Left Wingers have stock, too. However, even Left Wingers believe enough can be enough, and there are some cases where it just will not work. Here again, a bail out must be done in a way that is not just a blank check to the management of a floundering company. There have to be stipulations. God forbid, those stipulations drive Right Wingers crazy, but the government has to ensure that changes are being made to try to promote a recovery of the ailing company.

How do we build highways? The government takes bids and pays private companies to build these highways. Would we have an organized highway system without the government and without huge governmental spending? Is this socialism?

What about building a dam? What about an airport? What about a train station? What about a subway system? What about a huge football stadium? These are cooperative efforts between the government and private enterprise to help our economy.

Why can we not be realists? Our great country benefits from federal (and state) spending and its effects on a wide ranging assortment of our daily lives. It seems absurd to me to deny this. Our representatives must be more prudent with our tax dollars, but let's cut out the bombastic everyone is a pinko but me rhetoric. Let us work together. Children can do it; why do adults have so much trouble?

I occasionally risk obtaining the public moniker of an economic ignoramus, but let me just hint at an idea which makes sense to me. We are in a serious economic downturn. We (the government of, by, and for the people) can do a lot of things to try to stimulate the economy, or we can do absolutely nothing but cross our fingers and hope (the Rightie way). I think our government needs to be proactive, creative, far thinking, and realistic. Let us rely on history and the wonderful relationship between our government and our industry to work in partnership to get the economy going and create jobs, which will produce genuine improvements in the way we live. This requires spending money. It may increase the need for increasing taxes. The benefit would be to rebuild our aging infrastructure starting right now.

Why do I think that rebuilding our infrastructure starting right now is a good idea? First of all, some of our infrastructure is crumbling or is technologically outdated and needs updating, repairing, and replacing. Would we benefit as a country if we were able to rekindle our heavy industrial might? I think so. Do we think interest rates will continue to be this low forever? I think they will go up; how high and when is anyone's guess, but they will increase. So, borrow at historically low interest rates and invest in our country's future.

What kind of projects am I talking about? I am talking about big ones. I am not a technological wizard (which should be obvious by now), but I believe we should upgrade the way we distribute electricity within our electrical grid system to ensure a better, more efficient, safer from attack, long range project.

Should we not invest in alternative energy sources of all kinds? I think we should cover the gamut. We should invest in better, more efficient public energy generation, and we should invest in personal energy creation.

Why can't we live in a society where home owners can afford a home energy system that is affordable, environmentally friendly and aesthetically desirable?

What about a better rapid transit system? No, I am not trying to put airlines out of business; I am just trying to improve the transportation system.

In my opinion, the future of the United States of America being the world leader in technology and manufacturing must be facilitated to a large part by the cooperation between the government and our private sector. Some might call this socialism. **I call it the American Way.**

Our country is in a very precarious situation, at least in my opinion. While I do care about the debt crisis, I do not think it is the most daunting problem we face as a country. A much bigger problem is the problem facing a huge percentage of American workers who cannot find jobs that pay a livable wage.

We wring our hands about the 50% of the population who do not pay income taxes (they pay plenty of other taxes) and the 'whatever percentage' of the population that receives some type of federal assistance; yet the problem is much deeper and more insidious. Many hard-working employed people do not make enough money to live. That is the real crisis. This is a huge problem that third-world countries face. These third-world countries always seem to have the same economic structure: a small ultra-wealthy governing class, the plutocracy, and a huge low economic class with a small and struggling middle class.

This is the direction that I fear our country is headed. We do not need to worry about a European form of socialism; we need to worry about a Central and South American form of plutocracy. If enough Americans get to the point where they cannot support themselves, they will revolt. I mean violently, just like our south-of-the-border friends. If we do not figure out a strategy from the federal governmental level down, I see our country going into decline. We will lose our status as the greatest country in the world. This is not a problem that the states can handle. It is too big.

I absolutely do not believe that unregulated, private enterprise will solve this issue, in fact, I believe that unregulated private enterprise is the *biggest culprit* to this emerging problem.

We need to do some serious soul searching. **We need to buy American when we can.**

We need to create an environment where the American heavy industry can resurrect itself. We need to *stop* exporting many of our best jobs overseas. **We need a tax code that treats the wealthy and the middle class the same.**

Both parties had better come to recognize this problem or given enough time and continued decline of the middle class, we will insidiously become a third-world country.

Many jobs do not pay enough money for American workers to live. If our elected officials do not stand up for American workers, they eventually will stand up against those officials, and deservedly so.

Here we are again. The American way is for our government and our private enterprise to work together to solve these problems. The answers are not readily apparent. The commitment will be difficult, and it will take time. We are the government of and for the people. We are the People – all of us. Let us work together, quit sniping at each other, and commit to solving these difficult economic problems.

I encourage you to read the U.S. Constitution. Here is the Preamble. Left Wingers think this is beautiful.

> "We the People of the United States, in Order to form a more perfect Union, establish Justice, insure domestic tranquility, provide for the common defence, promote the general welfare, and secure the blessings of liberty to ourselves and our posterity, do ordain and establish this Constitution for the United States of America."

I have to talk about buying American. If you are going to agree with me on any one issue in this book, this is it: **Buy American.** I am talking about small, medium, and large purchases. I am not trying to put our foreign friends out of business; I am trying to help our own patriotic American businesses: management and labor. Let us put our money where our mouths are. Let's **buy American.** I am talking from booze to shoes. I am talking about boats to motorcycles. I am talking about ships and airplanes.

What I care about is buying American automobiles. Our government did the right thing when it bailed out General Motors. Is there anyone who really thinks that we should have let GM go out of business and let some foreign company come over and buy it up? Seriously, we are Americans. We should support America. We should demand the best products at the best prices. I want you to **buy American**. I want some of you brilliant entrepreneurs to figure out how to get American companies back into the television manufacturing business. I will **buy American**. I want American ingenuity to return to its dominant past. I want innovation. I want cooperation between management and labor and management and the government.

As a patriotic American, I demand it. You should too. **Buy American**!

Education

The public education of our children is the single most import role of state and local government. That should not be too big of a surprise to anyone, but it is a hallmark of Left Winger belief. Our children should be able to go to a good, safe public school and learn. This is a precious ideal to liberals. You will never find a Left Winger who wants to throw in the towel on public education and try to somehow privatize it.

I am not here to criticize private education at all. I am here to extol the virtue of public education and to tell one and all that we must remain vigilant in our efforts to protect that right.

One of the biggest problems facing the good people in the Great State of Texas is the argument over the quality of public education. I suspect that other states have similar problems, but Texas is what I know a little about and I will assume that the issues here in Texas are similar to those in other states. I am not here to tell anybody that public education could not and should not be better, much better, but I am here to tell you that it is one of the foundations upon which our democracy rests. Therefore, we must do everything we can to see that our children receive a high quality public education.

Why is the quality of public education in debate? There are a lot of reasons, and I am not here to debate all of them. I am here to talk about what I think Left Wingers can and should do to improve and preserve this wonderful institution. By the way, I invite all of your Right Wingers to help out as well.

I am not a researcher (that must be obvious by now), but I bet that most of the best public schools are located in the more affluent areas. If that is true, then what can and should be done to improve the quality of education in the schools in the less affluent areas?

Let us assume that more money will be a difficult commodity to procure. In my mind, there is no question that our educators need and deserve more money and better working conditions, but for this discussion let's leave money out of it.

What is it that makes the more affluent area schools better performing? The obvious reasons are that the neighborhoods are nicer looking, safer feeling, and have a much higher percentage of more educated families. I believe that in the classroom, children of educated people have a huge advantage over children of uneducated people.

There are other reasons, however, that make the more affluent schools better. One of those reasons is community involvement. In the wealthier school districts, the educated parents become involved in a hands on way. The parents, grandparents, and friends of the school are all over campus helping in every way they can. These people have time (perhaps because many are able to be stay-at-home parents), and they volunteer to help out the children, the teachers, and the administrators. The public education for these affluent kids is very good.

The obvious problem is how can we help the poorer neighborhood public schools. I think that we, as a society, should make a better volunteer effort to bolster every aspect and every program that is offered to these children. Sure, educators need more money and certainly enough money needs to be spent on poorer children in public schools to provide for the basic needs. I realize that in many places that there is insufficient money to even do that. However, public education in these poorer neighborhoods needs a much bigger effort. This problem should not be ignored.

I realize that I may sound like a Left Wing Polly Anna, but I really believe that volunteerism is a vital key in public schools. There are plenty of capable people who could be great volunteers and do a great job if they were motivated to do so and if they felt safe in doing so.

This brings me to my next point. If volunteers stay away from schools because they do not feel safe about the school area, what does that say about the safety of the children? We need more help from more people to help make our neighborhoods safe. We need our civic leaders pledging their time to help organize an army of volunteers to do everything they can do based upon their talents and desire to help the education process in our public schools in the poorer neighborhoods.

This volunteer effort is not going to be easy. It will need dedicated people who can set up volunteer organizations that will assess volunteers' abilities and interests and then place them in an area that is the best fit. Obviously, a person that cannot speak the Spanish language is not as well suited to help assist in the Spanish class. Some people may not have any academic skills whatsoever. Yet, if these people have a desire to volunteer, there are dozens of ways these people could be helpful. The scope of volunteerism must go from making the neighborhood safer and to keeping the campus safer so that other volunteers can feel safe about volunteering their skills and talents at the schools. Once the safety issue is improved and volunteers are out there keeping an eye out for lawbreakers, gangsters, dope dealers, and whoever else might be out there, then we can focus on other volunteers with more academic skills to these schools.

We can and must work together to improve the public education quality in our country. I do not mean to imply that all public schools in low income neighborhoods are performing on a substandard level. I am certain that there are many that are doing great. I say more power to those folks. I am only talking about the poorer public schools that perform poorly.

It seems to me that there should be very few public enterprises that are as important as educating our young people. This is even more so when we are talking about educating the less affluent children in our society. I mean, after all, if you are upper middle class and your child is performing poorly, you can send your child to a private school or hire a tutor or both. If you are poor, these options do not exist.

Are the answers easy, certainly not. Is the education of our children worth a Herculean effort, certainly so. Is it too much to think that Left Wingers and Right Wingers could unite on this issue? Heck no, let's get moving. Let us start now, right here, wherever you are. We have so many people who should be able to volunteer, let us encourage them, let us help them so that some day, the beneficiaries of our effort, our children, will benefit from a better education.

What are some simple suggestions? My friends will tell you that simple is all I have to offer, and I respond by saying that sometimes simple will get it done.

We need a committed and well organized effort that involves the teachers, the parents, the community, the school board, the police, volunteer organizations, the faith community, private enterprise, general do-gooders, and the government. What we do not need and what so often happens is that we find so much squabbling between all the groups that ought to be working together that nothing positive happens. Some people think that there is no hope for inner city public education. I disagree. The work is hard. It will take a lot of organization and effort, but it can happen. It needs to happen, and as a Left Winger, I am optimistic about seeing more and more commitment and more and more improvement.

Let us depart from problem schools and what we can do to improve them and talk about what needs to be taught. What should we be teaching in our public schools? Naturally we need to focus on basic education, but we must also teach all kinds of other lessons that one needs to really have an education.

I know this may sound silly to some of you, but a lot of people do not know how to use silverware. People do not know how a table should be set. How easy would it be to teach this? When I go out to lunch, I see all sorts of good people who would really benefit in the business world if they just had a little more confidence doing the smallest things like knowing how to hold a fork.

I am amazed how many people do not understand the importance of the magic words, please and thank you. I hope that public education instills this basic but so important part of life. I know almost all of us Left Wingers my age use the magic words, and I will have to admit my Right Winger friends do also.

On a more esoteric note, how many of you readers learned about money in school? I did not learn a darn thing about it, and I spent a long time in school. As it seems to be harder and harder to make appropriate plans for the future, it seems more and more important that children should be taught at a relatively young age (middle school or high school) about money management. Seriously, about the only education I ever had was the reminder that one should save for a rainy day. That is not enough. I think that our public schools ought to be teaching children about saving and investing. Let's raise children that are more business savvy than we were. We could have used more of this education, and they will almost certainly need it.

If the United States of America is to remain the greatest country in the world, we are going to need more emphasis on science and technology. We need to make those courses exciting and explain the cause and effect of understanding scientific and technical skills and how that translates into knowledge, power, and wealth. We need to have teachers in our public schools who can make these courses exciting, challenging, and worthwhile.

I read that many Chinese think that the United States is declining. While I want to dismiss that idea, I have to contemplate that it might be true. How can we reassert ourselves as a nation so that every nation knows who is number one now and for the future? I think a big part of the answer is better public education.

I realize that this is just a scratch of the surface about public education. I can only implore all of you to become involved with your neighborhood schools. I can assure you that it will be time well invested.

Since I started this book, the Great State of Texas has developed a shortfall in tax revenue. This occurred despite the fact that Texas is and has been run by Right Wingers for years and years. Whatever spending and taxing that occurs in Texas has been authorized or approved by Right Wingers. None the less, despite the conservative leadership which we have had in Texas for the last umpteen years, we are in a financial bind. I wonder how this could possibly happen to a state led by people who claim to be such ardent fiscal conservatives. My biggest criticism is not how in the world could all of you self-proclaimed expert, conservative, small government wizards let the Great State of Texas run into the ditch. It really is not.

My biggest criticism is how these Right Wingers are trying to get the Great State of Texas out of the financial ditch that they drove it into in the first place. That criticism is their decision to cut public educational funding. That makes me crazy! The explanation is that everyone must tighten their belts. My question is: "are our education belts not tight enough already? "

While all public educators and administrators certainly have an ongoing fiduciary responsibility to our taxpayers, we all have a fundamental responsibility to provide the highest quality of public education for our children in this great state. I do not believe that cutting funding to public education furthers the best interest of our children in this state.

Who gets hurt by cuts to public education? All of us get hurt directly or indirectly by this unwise decision. Can anyone think that increasing class size for our children is a good thing? That is a result of cutting state funding. Is cutting various programs a good idea? I think not.

Let us get down to brass tacks. Who is hurt directly, and who is hurt indirectly? The people who get hurt the most are the people who cannot afford the option of pulling their kids out of an overcrowded public school and placing their children into nice, private schools. Who falls into this category? Most Texans do, Righties and Lefties. Who is hurt the least? The Texans who can afford to put their kids in private schools.

Who else is hurt? All of us are hurt. How can the wealthy folks be hurt when they can afford to pay for a better private education than the rest of us? It is a little more attenuated, but it is a problem even for the wealthy. How can that be? Well, the wealthy people own businesses and are executives who earn big salaries and are entrepreneurs who make big money. Who are they going to hire to help them support their enterprises? They will have to hire less well-educated graduates from poorer public education. Or, I guess they can go to India and hire smart, well-educated Indian graduates to work in their businesses. Do you ever wonder how it is that the employers in United States of America have to go to India to hire qualified people to do technological work in American factories? Could the answer be that our public education system is not being nurtured enough? Think about it. Is India a better place to grow up and receive a public education? What the heck!

What about our civic leaders who try to woo companies from other states to the Great State of Texas. You can hear the pitch now, "Y'all come on down to Texas where taxes are low and public education is underfunded." That is an incentive if I have ever heard one! If businesses are less likely to come to Texas, that slows down the economy, which reduces our tax base, which causes more short falls, which drives us deeper into the financial ditch, which is obviously bad for everyone, even rich people, regardless of political affiliation.

I can hear the hollering now. You Left Wing so in so, what would you do to save money? Well, surprise, I have an idea or two. As I mentioned, I used to be a prosecutor in the Dallas County District Attorney's Office. Let's trim some money from law enforcement that is wasted, at least in my opinion. Tomorrow let us decriminalize marijuana. Let us tax it. I think that the idea of medical marijuana is a joke. Sure, it may be helpful for people who have certain medical conditions but come on, medicinal marijuana? Let us call it what it is, a drug that gets people high. If we legalize marijuana tomorrow, will the world end? If we legalize marijuana tomorrow, will we generate more tax revenue? In 2009, how much tax revenue was collected from the taxation of cigarettes in the United States of America? Take a guess...over 17 billion dollars.

According to the Center for Disease Control, cigarette smoking was estimated to be responsible for $193 billion in annual health-related economic losses in the United States ($96 billion in direct costs and $97 billion in lost productivity). Smoking tobacco is bad, but we are taxing it like mad.

What do you think the United States would save by ceasing to spend law enforcement resources on marijuana enforcement: countless police man hours, savings on jail space, savings on court appointed attorneys who represent the people who get arrested and savings on probation supervision.

What would the United States receive by legalizing marijuana? How much tax revenue would be raised? Would it be twice the amount raised by taxation on cigarettes, would it be five times, would it be ten times, would it be more? Could the tax revenue on marijuana sales exceed $200,000,000,000? It sounds so far-fetched, but if you think about the price of cigarettes compared to the price of illegal marijuana, the numbers are a little mind boggling.

There would be other benefits, also. If we license the growing, sale, and distribution of marijuana in the United States, it will put Mexican marijuana cartels out of business. It will cut down on drug violence; at least that which pertains to marijuana.

It will eliminate the hypocrisy that alcohol and cigarettes are fine/legal and marijuana is bad/illegal. What college-aged person in the United States does not know that?

Some people will assert that marijuana is a gateway to other drug usage and, therefore, it should remain illegal. Fair enough, let us assume that it is some type of gateway. Is it really a gateway? Is it the only gateway? What about alcohol or tobacco? Should we criminalize them because they may be a gateway to other drug usage? We have tried to prohibit the sales of alcohol, and it was a disaster. I do not recall a legal ban on tobacco sales and possession; one may have existed, however, the issue at hand is whether we should legalize marijuana. It seems obvious to me that the societal risk/reward tips overwhelmingly toward legalization.

Am I telling everyone to get involved in some type of reefer madness? Of course not. I am just telling you the truth. I am not a fan of marijuana, but I might give up cigars for marijuana if it were legal.

Let us look into our prisons and try to figure out how many of the people serving time are doing so for drug possession who do not pose a danger to the rest of us. Parole those folks, save money.

Almost all people who are placed on misdemeanor probation are assigned a probation officer and required to report to that probation officer as a condition of probation. Good grief, this is a huge waste of time and money. Let the probation officers spend their time supervising felons; those are the serious criminals who need supervision.

Let law enforcement officers spend their time looking for dangerous people, not pot heads. Let's supervise those people on felony probation, not misdemeanor probation. Let's quit warehousing people who are in prison for drug possession and are not a danger to society. Let's take the money we save and the taxes we generate from these ideas and put it back into the public education fund. Let's use these savings and revenues on our children's public education.

There may be some cynics out there who think that this Left Winger is already smoking dope. These cynics may think that if we legalize marijuana it will be impossible to teach all those stoned kids in school. Guess what, if you think that, you may not understand what kids are doing already.

I know that most of you reading this book have never considered being an activist. If you are going to consider activism, think about educational activism to support public schools. Think about it. It is worth the investment of your time, your energy, and yes, your taxes. The future of America is dependent on our public education system. We owe it to our children, and we owe it to ourselves, to see that our public education is the best in the world.

Government

Despite what your Right Winger friends say at cocktail parties, there is a real and legitimate need for government. Our government, the Government of the United States of America, is really you and me: left, right, center, apathetic, energetic, and every other kind of person there is. In fact, our government is overwhelmingly a good thing. It amazes me every time I hear a Right Winger bellow how bad our government is. We have the best government in the world.

What should the government do? Left Wingers will honestly admit that the government has a large and important roll in the lives of every American. After all, what is it that makes our government work but our laws and the people working within those laws to make this great country of ours work? Right Wingers disingenuously tell anyone that will listen that the government is a monolithic entity operating with the sole purpose of making our lives worse. In fact, the opposite is true. Right Wing logic is so transparent. They want people to believe that honest people get elected, and as soon as they assume the mantle of a public official, they become part of some evil empire. I assume that they make exceptions for the Right Wingers that are in government when they are standing in their presence, but you all know what I mean.

What is the roll of the federal government? Simply speaking, it runs the show. When foreigners talk about America, they are talking about the American Federal Government in Washington D. C. Usually, they mean the executive branch, but they talk about the government. The President sets the tone for the Federal Government, both domestically and on issues of foreign policy. In my opinion, the President is the most powerful man in the world. I think Right Wingers agree with me on this issue.

I plan on talking a lot about different aspects of the policies of the government later in the book. Right now, I just want to expose the tip of the iceberg, so to speak.

The government of the United States is not evil. We do a lot of things that are wrong, but we do not have an evil government. There are mean-spirited people that are elected to represent us, but the government itself is not evil. If a Right Winger starts to rant about the how evil this or that is, tell him or her to lighten up.

Naturally, I believe that our government would be operating much better if we had a majority of Left Wingers in there, but I will wait to be vindicated on this opinion.

I am always amazed when I hear an otherwise intelligent friend of mine opine on the virtues of everything to do with private enterprise and the baseness of anything to do with government enterprise. There are so many functions of government that work as well or better than private enterprise that it should be obvious to even the rightest of Right Wingers. The list is long.

The endeavor of our police officers and fire fighters goes without question. Have you ever heard a Right Winger say, "Dang it, I sure wish we had some private security types to capture dangerous felons"? Do they say, "I bet those building owners could put out that fire faster than those firefighters"? I doubt that even the rightest of Right Wingers will say that. Folks, the police and the firefighters are part of the government. Granted this is local government, but it is government.

How about our soldiers? Do Right Wingers think mercenaries or contractors can defend us against foreign attack better than our military? Can a bunch of gun-wielding rednecks defeat Al-Qaeda? The military is a part of the federal government.

I might add that since I started writing this book, Osama Bin Laden has been hunted down and killed. This happened because of the cooperation of our President, his staff, the C.I.A, the military support, and the Navy Seals. All of these people are employees (yikes!) of the federal government of the United States of America. This is a time in our history when I believe most Americans feel a sense of satisfaction that justice has been served. The justice was brought about not by private enterprise, but by the might of the United States government. It must gag some Right Wingers to have to acknowledge that justice was served by a Left Wing President.

Do Right Wingers think that instead of our federal government, we should have a board of directors made up of the largest shareholders of the largest companies enact our laws?

Does unregulated, private industry have a history concerning environmental protection of which it can be proud?

Should we disempower our government so that it cannot prevent monopolies?

I can go on and on, but I hope the point is made. The government does a lot of things better than the private sector.

So, does that mean that Left Wingers are a bunch of communists that loathe the private sector? Despite what the deluded Right thinks, of course not! Left Wingers value work and being productive. We want good, well paying jobs. We want an honest day's pay for an honest day's work. As I have already mentioned, if you work for a living, you probably have a lot more in common with the Left than the Right, even though you may not realize it yet. (After all, it is still pretty early in the book).

Left Wingers want responsible management in our corporations and our businesses. We want productive labor. We want our businesses to be the best, most productive, and profitable in the world. That is what Left Wingers want out of the private sector. Left Wingers understand that in this great country there must be cooperation between government and the private sector. Neither is inherently evil; both are essential to our American way of life.

In my opinion, the Hand of God guided our forefathers as they struggled to create this great country. As I said earlier, they made a lot of mistakes, but they came through big time in establishing the freest country on the planet. (The freest, at least if you were not a slave). Friends, these guys were not Right Wingers that wanted to keep the status quo. These people were Left Wingers who had a great vision that they were able to realize. When I think about this effort, it brings tears to my eyes. These were great men doing great things that have profoundly altered the course of history.

What did these men do? They created the greatest government the world has ever seen. They truly understood that the government should be created by and for the people. They understood that the government could become tyrannical, and they wrote laws to protect us from tyranny. God bless them. They understood the balance of power. That is why we have three branches of government: for checks and balances, to see that the greatest good is done for the greatest number of Americans, and to see that the rights guaranteed under our Constitution and Bill or Rights are protected.

This is not an indictment on free enterprise, but free enterprise is focused on making money, not protecting our fundamental rights.

So, we have the greatest government in the history of the world. Left Wingers will sing the praises of our government and extol its wonder and virtue. Left Wingers will also acknowledge that it is not perfect, and it needs constant attention and work. It will not remain great if our citizens become apathetic or antagonistic toward it. We love America. We love and respect our Constitution.

Left Wingers love the rights that we have. We love the opportunity that we have. We love our freedom. We honor those who have bravely served our country; fighting to preserve these rights and our way of life.

Do Right Wingers love our country? It seems that all I hear on conservative talk shows is hatred of our government; hatred of this policy or that policy; hatred of this or that law; hatred of this or that elected official. Why do we hear so much hate spewing from these Right Wing commentators? I believe that it is a terrible appeal to the most despicable personality traits that people have. Unfortunately, it gets ratings. Does it help anyone but those commentators and the sycophants who benefit from those rants? I absolutely do not believe it. However, do I believe that Right Wingers love our Country? Yes, I do.

Do I think that many good people have been bamboozled into some sort of inane frenzy? Yes, I do. I hope that reasonable conservative people will retake conservative ideology from those who are mongers of hate.

Do Right Wingers love the government? Sure they do, however, they are just afraid to say so, because they are afraid that they will be humiliated by some extremist who questions their commitment to the Right Wing cause. If they really hated the government as much as they claim, none would ever run for office. The truth is that they are running for political office, and they do love the government and America as much as the Left Wingers do.

Foreign Policy

The idea that I might write a comprehensive and interesting chapter about foreign policy is completely unreasonable, and I do not plan to wear you out with any attempt to do so. Instead, I will try to briefly discuss when and why the United States of America should use its armed forces. I will also discuss what I believe should be a huge shift in our economic foreign policy, which emphasizes a dramatic reduction of the exportation of American jobs.

Let us start off with the use of force issue. Although President George W. Bush called himself a "Compassionate Conservative," (which is a form of Right Wingism), I am willing to concede that the Bush administration made many moves that could not be considered either conservative or liberal. I would argue that they were just generally wrong. I again want to thank my friend, Sted Garber, a genuine conservative for helping me with this particular issue. My inclination was to throw conservatives into the "Bush Briar Patch" foreign policy mess, and he convinced me that real conservatives do not agree with President Bush's foreign policy either. As I do not really want to bash President Bush or his administration, I will charge forward into the fray and discuss Left Wing foreign policy.

Left Wingers think that our interests and the interests of the world are best served when we to try to achieve a win-win foreign policy as opposed to a win-lose foreign policy. This means that we should negotiate with all countries in an effort to achieve some sort of mutually beneficial relationship. We must keep open discussions with friends *and foes* alike all the time. The idea that we should thrust our chests out and declare that we will not talk to this leader or that leader is just not good politics or foreign policy.

The world political situation is constantly changing. We must be willing to change with the times and try to anticipate these changes so that we can be at the forefront of these political changes and assume our rightful position as the world leader. We talk about a world economy and the interrelated nature of world politics, and we must have a government that can adapt to these changes and lead the charge for a better life for Americans and others in other countries around the world. This requires letting bygones be bygones. This also means trying to work with other leaders as opposed to trying to antagonize or demonize them. Frankly, demonizing others seems pretty stupid to me unless, of course, they really are demons.

Think about it. Germany and Japan were our most hated enemies of the twentieth century; yet, both of them are our allies today. In World War II, we were engaged in a fight to the finish and, thank God, we were victorious. Vietnam is not too dissimilar, either. Today, somehow, the USA and Vietnam seem to get along just fine. I do not want to get into the quagmire of whether Vietnam was a just war or not. That issue is for others, not me. I bring this up only to emphasize the importance of flexibility in our foreign policy. Yesterday's enemies may be today's friends, and today's friends may be tomorrow's enemies.

President Barack Obama indicated that he would be willing to negotiate with any country, friend or enemy. Wow, did this cause a media fracas or what? I have to say that I was disappointed at some of my Lefty friends on this issue, too. People were howling that it would be a disgrace to the dignity of the office for the President of the USA to negotiate with some enemy dictator. This was an amazing reaction to me. If you have confidence in your President, (and if we have a Left Winger President, who in their right mind would not?), then who is in a better position to engage in negotiations than the President? Now, are these negotiations always successful? Of course they are not always successful, but what is a better alternative? Should the President send a political lackey to do his or her bidding? Is there historic precedent for Presidential negotiations with our enemies? What about Eisenhower and Khrushchev; what about Kennedy and Khrushchev, Nixon and Mao, Reagan and Gorbachov? There are numerous examples of this type of high level debate. Not all have gone smoothly or been successful, but the idea of negotiating seemed better to these Presidents than duking or nuking it out. I am baffled that anyone could even argue this point with a straight face. Obama was right, and Obama is a Left Winger. Winston Churchill is credited with saying, "Jaw jaw is better than war war." Nobody would call Churchill a wimp.

In my opinion, Right Wingers have a misguided sense of international cooperation, at least in my mind. They seem to think that in WWI and WWII, the USA got involved and every other allied country just sat back and said "sic 'em," while the good ole' USA whipped enemy rear without any help at all. That is not the way it was. We had a lot of allies in both wars, and whether we could have prevailed without any help is academic at best because we did receive a lot of military help in both cases. If you do not believe this, call a German friend and ask if the Russians had anything to do with the allied victory in World War II.

In Operation Desert Storm, our president, George H. W. Bush, correctly believed that a real coalition was needed to achieve the military and political objective that he outlined. Whether one agrees with the wisdom of entering the conflict once again is the not the purpose of this opinion. The purpose is that President George H. W. Bush understood that real political and military cooperation was essential to his goal. My belief is that President George H. W. Bush made a wise choice to seek and obtain significant international support both of a military and political nature.

Unfortunately, President George W. Bush made many bad and unilateral decisions in his quest to make war in Iraq and Afghanistan. Here is a big debate. Some of my Right Winger friends swear at President George W. Bush for his poor decision making and implementation of his war effort as well as the squandering of the good will that all America and most of the free world shared with the United States after September 11, 2001. All of my Left Winger friends also harshly criticize the Bush administration. However, some of my Right Winger friends believe that President George W. Bush is and will be considered one of the greatest presidents in our history. Go figure this. I know it is weird, but I swear it is true. I am not going to mention any of their names because they are my friends and they may change their minds before this book gets published, and I do not want to embarrass any of them.

I think that most of my Right Winger friends think that Left Wingers are pathetic, pacifist pukes who would not fight to save their souls. I gotta say, "That is wrong my friend!" Left Wingers are ready, willing, and able to go to war when and only when it is the last option. However, if that occurs, Left Wingers believe that to commit to war is to commit to a reign of hell on the enemy. War is really hell on earth. It is cruel, it is catastrophic, it is sacrificial, it is bloody, it is chaotic and it is a struggle to the finish. There is no such thing to a Left Winger as mission accomplished until the enemy has been totally defeated and surrendered unconditionally.

There is no reason to go to war unless it is the last option and is essential to the safety of the United States. There must be a commitment to fight it out with all resources that are available. The cost of war will be high. There must be an understanding that there will be a loss of precious American lives. There must be an understanding that there will be lots of enemy casualties. There must be an understanding that many, many innocent men, women, and children will be killed in a horrible way. That is the nature of war. Americans must be committed to accept these terrible consequences before going to war. We need volunteerism. We may need to reinstate the draft. There is no such thing as a nice war. War is horrible. The aftermath of war will be staggering. What we choose to do after we have totally destroyed the capacity and will of our enemy has to be planned out.

Hopefully, we will never need to commit to an all out war again. If we do, I can assure you that it will not be undertaken without a great amount of thought, preparation, and prayer. I believe that we will prevail. God help any potential enemy because if war does breaks out, that enemy will be devastated by the armed forces of the United States of America.

I realize that there may be times where we may have to commit troops in harms way without the need or declaration of war. Once again, I think that the Left Winger does not engage in this type of military action lightly either. The same principles apply. Appropriate and overwhelming force brought forth to annihilate the enemy causing a minimum number of American casualties and a maximum amount of enemy casualties is essential in an effort to accomplish this objective. Some Left Wingers are pacifists, but most are not. As you now know, we will fight, and we will fight to the finish.

Let us talk a little about the Obama administration's effort to find and kill Osama Bin Laden. Prior to this military action, Right Wingers assailed Obama as a "Do nothing political novice who had no idea how to do anything on a military basis." They just thought that since "W" could not get Bin Laden, he could not get got. Some Righties were so dumbfounded when they learned that Bin Laden had been killed that they refused to give the credit to the Obama administration. It was almost crazy to listen to the explanations that these haters of Obama made to try to minimize the success of the Navy Seals who executed such a daring plan, and the Obama administration that authorized it.

This criticism, while American in its basis of freedom of speech, was clearly anti-American, and these critics should be ashamed. The elimination of the most infamous and most heinous American-hating terrorist in the world should have been cheered by every American. Those who belittled the President's efforts are petty.

Now that I have calmed down a little, I want to talk about how our foreign policy should promote American jobs. Let us start by addressing the issue of job exportation. As a fine Left Winger, I am against sending good jobs out of the USA. Heck, we are Americans and I want us to have the first shot at the best jobs in the world. It is a big philosophical and political argument over who benefits more from the exportation of good jobs to foreign countries. Lefties believe that large corporations and their shareholders benefit from the exportation of jobs from the USA where higher wages must be paid to foreign countries where lower wages can be paid. Granted, a lot of Left Wingers own stock, just like Right Wingers, but Left Wingers oppose job exportation.

As I see it, this is the situation. One can make a tennis shoe in Malaysia for ten dollars, and send it over here and sell it for one hundred dollars. Maybe it costs eighty dollars to make it in the USA, and if it sells for the same one hundred dollars, it is easy to see why big corporations want to export those jobs. But, and this is a big but, what is the long-term affect of exporting these tennis shoe jobs? American tennis shoe laborer loses his job and the American shoe manufacturer has to charge more, pay less or go out of business. Do we need a domestic tennis shoe industry? It is essential to the American way of life? Maybe some of us will say that we can live without an American tennis shoe manufacturing industry. What about the clothing industry, in general? What about the toy industry? What about the pineapple industry. What about the automobile manufacturing industry? Try to find a television that is manufactured in the United States; I bet you cannot do it. I could not!

It does not seem to take a genius to see that eventually we could export darn near every good job somewhere to have it made cheaper so that a corporation could have a higher profit margin. How can that be bad? Well, if we send out all the good jobs, who is going to have enough money to buy the product that these companies want to sell? What about the American laborer? Will the American laborer have a job or enough money to buy these goods? Maybe not. That, my friends, is bad. No, it is not bad; it would foretell the collapse of this great country. It is disastrous.

Let us assume that you are a really hard-shell free trader and you think that Adam Smith's "Invisible Hand" will somehow move around the jobs so that everyone will have to evolve to keep up. Wonderful world competition should make better products at a better price. Even a Left Winger has to say that this sounds good, at least superficially. The problem needs a slightly deeper look. Yes, the idea of world-wide unfettered free trade sounds *soooo* good. The problem is that it is too good to be true.

Does the free trader want to export *every* job that can be done cheaper to a foreign country? Look at the money that could be saved? What about our national interest? What about public policy? What about providing a good job at a good wage for Americans? Yes, Americans who pay taxes, educate our children, serve as police and fire fighters, and volunteer for the military. Do we as a country have an obligation to those people? What about every other hard working American? How dependent does the free trader want us to be on our trading allies?

Let us take the Chinese for an example. Should we send our weapons technology over there? They can build weapons cheaper than we can. Should we send our automotive industry over there? They can build vehicles cheaper than we can. What about warships, military aircraft, submarines, helicopters; you name it, and they can build it cheaper.

Now, let us say that we have sent the majority of our nationally sensitive industry to China. Let us further assume that the corporations are having record profits from the sales of these important products. This sounds great for the corporations, their corporate officers, the employees who still work in the United States, and their shareholders. Yippee! This company and that are making bigger profits than ever. Year after year of financial joy! Stocks are soaring and the economic sky seems as if it will be blue forever.

Oops. What happens if the United States gets into a snit with China? What the heck are we going to do? Ask China for some cruise missiles in case we need to duke it out? Oh, you say, that will not happen because we will keep those jobs and that industry over here and not get ourselves into that bind. OK, fair enough, but really where would you draw the line?

Who draws the line? Should the corporate magnates who have a fiduciary obligation to their shareholders make the decision as to what industries should be exported? Should organized labor make that decision? Should we rely on the good old idea of supply and demand? Who should decide where the jobs and industry of American companies should be? I am not so naïve that I do not understand the idea that foreign companies can produce this or that cheaper than we can. I also know that these foreign companies can make very fine products. If Americans buy cheaper and comparable quality goods from foreign companies, it makes sense that the American manufacturer will eventually go out of business.

What should we do? I would say we need a much more level playing field. Instead of our companies conceding that we cannot manufacture goods in the USA as cheap as we could in another country and, therefore, we must export jobs. we should look at why that problem exists. What do almost 100% of my Right Wing friends say the problems are? Come on you know what they are going to say: "Labor Unions and personal injury lawyers, whom many consider to be the worst of all the anti-American Left Wingers on the planet." Fair enough, I will tell you right now that I am a personal injury lawyer. So having revealed that bit of information, let us sally forward.

I would agree that the cost of lawsuits raises the costs of goods and services. I am not going to battle this issue out right here, but let me agree that it does. I would also say that these lawsuits force companies to make safer and better products, which benefit all Americans. (Sorry, I could not help myself).

Now, let me talk about American labor. Is it more expensive than labor in other parts of the world? Yes, of course. Should it be? Yes, it should. Why should it cost more? It should cost more because we put a lot into our labor force, and we expect a lot from our labor force.

Should American laborers be able to expect some type of health insurance or, perhaps, universal health care? Heck yes they should! Should a laborer be able to expect that he or she should be fairly compensated if he or she is injured while working? Absolutely. These are benefits that separate us from third-world labor centers. These expectations, when realized, cost money.

Left Wingers believe that working people in the USA should be protected from practices that are unreasonably dangerous.

If a worker is in the course and scope of his or her employment and he or she is injured by the negligence of the employer, then that employer should compensate the injured worker for medical bills, lost wages, impairment, physical pain, mental anguish, and disfigurement. Left Wingers believe that workers are human beings and need to have rights to be able to safely pursue a career. I think that Right Wingers agree with this idea also. The difference is how lefties and righties deal with this issue.

Labor in the countries where we are exporting these jobs do not have the rights and protections that we enjoy here. If you are injured in many countries where jobs are exported and you cannot work, it is just "tough stuff." That injured worker cannot expect to receive healthcare or compensation for lost wages or for any impairment. If that injured worker is really hurt badly and cannot work again, the American company has no obligation whatsoever. A company can save a lot of money. What is the human cost? Apparently, in many countries, it does not matter. If our corporations export manufacturing jobs to these countries where workers are not provided benefits, it does not matter to our corporations either.

What about child labor in these countries? Is that important to us? Gosh, children in third-world countries will probably work for less than adults in third-world countries. Should we hire children? Should they work sixty, seventy, or eighty hours a week? These are important issues. Should we just send the jobs over and close our eyes to the working conditions of the laborers over there just to make more money over here?

What about the manufacture of hazardous materials or the use of hazardous materials in the manufacturing process? In the USA, we have learned some hard lessons about the long-term effects of hazardous materials. We have enacted laws that almost everyone thinks are in the best interest of our citizens for our protection from this type of exposure. When a company knowingly fails to comply with those standards, the government comes in and puts the kibosh on it and the personal injury lawyers come in and start suing. This is to protect us from us. In many foreign countries, these protections do not exist.

How does a little contamination in some other country affect us? I can think of two ways. When we purchase contaminated products manufactured in another country, we get contaminated. This is bad. If the other country has no regulations protecting the environment from contamination, the contaminated products and materials contaminate the world's environment. That is bad also.

Does the environment really matter in some other country? Certainly it does. If we sit back and let other countries pollute their water and their polluted water flows into the oceans, it stands to reason that the oceans will become polluted. If the oceans become too polluted, then we have a potential worldwide catastrophe. The same rule applies to air pollution.

If other countries that have cheap labor and are producing goods bound for the USA are poor environmental shepherds, we need to do something. I would suggest advising these countries to improve their environmental awareness. If that does not occur, then cease trading with them. If that does not do it, then we need to flex more muscle. Get our first-world allies to cease trading with them. The environment is important to every soul on the planet. Our health is important. Our children's health is even more important.

Our labor force is important to the future of our country. Not everyone will be a lawyer or white-collar worker. We need laborers. We need to protect their jobs for their future, for our future, and for the future of the United States of America. American labor must earn a fair wage so that American workers can afford to enjoy life, liberty, and the pursuit of happiness. This is an issue about which I feel a great amount of passion. I could write enough to really wear you out and bore those of you who are kind enough to still be reading. I will sum this up. **You need to buy American made products**. We need to keep American jobs in America.

The Environment

This is one of the great topics for Left Winger versus Right Winger cocktail debates. It also is one of the most important issues facing our government and the world. What do Left Wingers think about the environment? Once again, there are a lot of lefties out there who probably cover a lot of ground, but I am going to make a stab at what I think Left Wingers generally think. We generally think that the earth has been a great place to live, and we want to keep it that way. We realize that human activity certainly can put a scar on the planet, and we should be prudent with our natural resources: earth, air, water, plant life, fossil fuels, and other elements and chemicals. I suspect that most Right Wingers would generally agree with this idea. As they say, "The devil is in the details."

This Left Winger believes that the population explosion is the biggest drain on our natural resources. Unfortunately, as countries develop and increase in population, they use more and more resources and tend to destroy more and more of the earth's natural resources. Many of us believe that voluntary population growth reduction is essential to the long-term salvation of the natural beauty and resources of our planet. The United Nations has published a report that states that the world population has more than doubled in the last sixty years from less than three billion people to more than six billion.

How many people is six billion? How long a line would six billion people make if you lined them shoulder to shoulder? Let's assume that each person is about one foot from shoulder to shoulder. This line would be six billion feet long. How long is that? It is 1,136,364 miles long. We could stretch to the moon and back two times and have plenty more length. That is a 480,000 mile round trip! That is a lot of people living on our planet.

I am concerned with the growth of our cities and the destruction of our natural environment. When I was a boy, we used to drive from north Austin to Round Rock (Texas, of course) to visit my great uncle. We drove out in the country and passed field after field. It was verdant, and it was beautiful. Today, Round Rock is a suburb of Austin. I am certain that all of you folks that are my age or older have similar stories to tell. I love Austin and Round Rock for that matter, but we are turning fields into concrete and asphalt. There has been a huge population growth in the last fifty years. Miles and miles of ranchland and farmland have been converted into roads, highways, strip centers, office buildings, and residential developments. What will our country look like in fifty or one hundred years? There is not an unlimited amount of land. Take a trip to Galveston. Twenty years ago there were all sorts of open beaches, and now the entire island is filling up with beach houses and condos. How long will it be before our coastline looks like a human wall of construction? I guess everybody that wants to have the ability to have an unobstructed ocean view had better buy a place soon because we are running out of beach.

What about the tree hugger element of the Left Wing? I am somewhat of a tree hugger. I am thankful that our government has saved the giant sequoias from being chopped down so that generation after generation can appreciate their grandeur.

I once thought that conservatives wanted to conserve. Truthfully, I think a lot of them still do want to preserve our natural resources. I hope that our elected leaders can help save our wilderness from overdevelopment. Can you imagine canyon-side condominiums on the Grand Canyon, office buildings towering over the Gettysburg Battlefield, or a bunch of fast food restaurants on top of Mt. Rushmore? I hope not. I want our grandchildren and their grandchildren to have a country that has beautiful wilderness and marvelous national parks. Is this really only a Left Wing idea?

Let's talk about oil; black gold, the "Texas T." Do we need it? Heck yes, we do. Do we need a lot of it? Heck yes, we do. Do we need to free ourselves of the shackles of dependency on Middle Eastern oil? Is there anyone who thinks we do not? So what is the best thing to do? Should we do more drilling? Should we spend more money researching and developing alternative energy sources? The answer is yes to both. The problem is that we spend way too little of our collective time and energy trying to produce alternative energy sources. A friend of mine, Sted Garber, who is the retired CEO of the world's largest offshore drilling company, told me that he did not think we would ever run out of oil. It will just get more and more expensive to find. In his opinion, as the price of oil increases, then the natural response is for free enterprise to work harder to develop price competitive alternative energy sources. As he told me, when mankind progressed from the stone age to the iron age, it was not because they were running out of stone. I agree with my friend a great deal.

I think that the government, the academic community, and the free enterprisers need to put a lot more time, energy, and money into the development of alternative energy sources.

The global warming issue is very perplexing to me. If anyone is a clear thinker, he or she should at least think of the ramifications of global warming. Yet, is seems to me that a lot of Righties are not interested in worrying one bit about the possible catastrophic consequences of long-term global warming. They seem to spend their energy telling anyone who will listen (other Righties) that global warming is some kind of Left Wing conspiracy to allow the federal government to tax us more and somehow enslave us. You know the old story, global warming is hokum, and the only people who believe it are big government liberals who want to do this or do that: increase the size of government and impose taxes on hard-working patriotic Americans. This is so reactionary. It seems that Righties reason that liberals must have come up with any study that implies that the earth is getting warmer, and since it was some liberal who did the research, it must be a lie.

What I do not hear from my Right Wing friends is that global warming is a reality and that it poses potentially dire massive environmental and economic consequences.

A recent study may indicate that at least some Righties are coming around on this important issue.

The Berkeley Earth Study is the biggest climate study to date, and one of the individuals who participated in the study was Dr. Richard Muller. In October 2011, Muller recanted his global warming skepticism in an op-ed in the Wall Street Journal, writing the following:

"When we began our study, we felt that skeptics had raised legitimate issues, and we didn't know what we'd find. Our results turned out to be close to those published by prior groups. We think that means that those groups had truly been very careful in their work, despite their inability to convince some skeptics of that. They managed to avoid bias in their data selection, homogenization and other corrections.

Global warming is real. Perhaps our results will help cool this portion of the climate debate. How much of the warming is due to humans and what will be the likely effects? We made no independent assessment of that."

I assume there will always be people who still think the world is flat and that global warming does not exist. I do not think you will find any Left Wingers who hold those beliefs. The issue is what should we do about global warming? Ignore it like a smaller and smaller group of Righties encourage? Cross our fingers and hope that it goes away? Engage the collective American and world-wide genius to develop plans to reduce global warming and to prepare for the ramifications of global warming if it cannot be abated? I think that most of the complex problems facing the world can be simplified and that with a big and concerted effort, great things can happen. After all, this is the only country that has ever put a man on the moon.

Surely protecting our air, water, and other natural resources is as important to Righties as it is to Lefties. The fundamental problem that reasonable Right Wing thinkers have is that they must acknowledge that this is a problem that must be tackled in a coordinated and world-wide effort, which will require governments to act together. This runs contrary to their idea that government is almost always bad, to which Left Wingers disagree.

Is it too much to ask that our government and private enterprise work together to encourage research and development of all kinds of energy-saving ideas? Sure, money is being spent and people are working, but is this not an extremely high priority?

God bless those people whose answer to solve the energy crisis is "drill baby drill." It is one of those adages which sounds so simple and so true that one could wonder why it has not occurred, and why have we not been saved from the clutches of OPEC, which controls such a huge percentage of the world's current oil supplies and is not exactly the best friend of the old USA?

Unfortunately, it is not the end-all answer to all of our energy problems. If we had a lot more domestic (good old American) oil, certainly we would be less dependent on OPEC, but we would be avoiding the real issue, which is how to be more energy efficient. We must reduce the effects of the internal combustion engine on our environment, and we must pursue a greater variety of energy producing technologies that could have a much less negative impact on our air and water.

As an example, the government has issued mandates that automobile manufacturers must meet as it relates to fuel economy. The idea is that we would need less fuel if our vehicles were more fuel efficient. Sounds like a good idea to me. I looked up the standards, and they were too complicated for me to be able to understand well enough to write about in this book in a way that would be half way interesting. But the idea is important.

Have our domestic automobile manufacturers used the best minds they have to make more fuel-efficient vehicles since the first oil crisis in 1973? No, they have not. However, recently great strides are being made here and abroad and gas mileage is improving! This is good. Imagine if you purchased a vehicle (preferably made by American union workers) which got fifty percent better gas mileage than your last vehicle. And let's project that the overwhelming majority of Americans did the same thing. In ten years, we would need significantly less oil from OPEC without doing anything else.

Also, new homes are more fuel efficient than older homes. Let us assume that this trend not only continues but that homes become dramatically more fuel efficient. Let us also assume that more and more incentives are given to home owners to refit older homes with more fuel efficient systems. Let's keep going and assume that this happens in commercial construction and retrofitting. The big picture would be less and less need for oil. I am not saying oil is bad; I am saying that we can be more efficient and use less of it and make what we have last longer. If the demand falls (if you believe in supply and demand), the price could actually go down, and we would be free of OPEC!

If we use our technology to create motors and engines that deliver similar or more power with considerably less oil being burned, we get the additional benefit of a cleaner environment. Is this only important to liberals? Surely not; it is important to all of us.

Having a better quality of air and water for future generations of Americans is important. Lowering our need for dependence on foreign oil is important. Paying a smaller percentage of our incomes on energy is important. We must have the determination and cooperation to move forward. Is it going to cost money? Sure it is – lots of money. Is it worth it? How can we not afford to stay as the world's technological leader. Decisions we make now will have long-term consequences on our environment. Let's work together and make the right ones. We should demand better technology for a better environmental tomorrow. We can do it.

Taxes

What is it about taxes that makes Right Wingers believe that they understand everything about them and that Left Wingers do not understand anything about them? Frankly, I am not sure that I can answer that question, but all Left Wingers understand this feeling.

Just like almost every other issue I discuss in this book, I am no expert on the Internal Revenue Code, and I am not certain that anyone really is. I took an income tax class in law school, and it almost killed me. I have a lot of respect for those tax professionals who toil with the code and try to figure this or that out and try to help their clients so that they do not over pay their taxes.

As I have mentioned, I am no tax expert; however, that certainly will not keep me from venturing into this issue. (This is part of my "write first and think later mentality," which is something I know I share with my Right Wing friends).

Why do Right Wingers believe that Left Wingers want to give all of everyone's money to the government in the form of taxes? Right Wingers seem to believe that by doing so, Left Wingers will somehow empower themselves and be able to enslave Right Wingers into a form of economic servitude that rewards the wicked and slovenly and punishes the righteous and industrious. Does that sum it up?

I realize that this is an exaggeration, but we hear it all the time to a greater or lesser degree: "You Left Wingers are pinkos who want to ruin our great country by taxing us to death."

Let us think about this. Let us calm down. At this point, the Left Wingers who are reading this are mad and the Right Wingers feel some kind of something, but I am not sure what.

Hear the truth: Left Wingers do not like paying taxes either! Oh my gosh, call EMS! Right Wingers are having fits everywhere because they think it is a lie! It is not a lie! It is the truth. Nobody likes paying taxes. Everybody thinks the government wastes money. Everyone thinks the government is funding pork projects that only benefit their cronies. Funny thing is that everyone is both Lefties and Righties.

Why do Right Wingers think they are so right and that Left Wingers are so wrong? Maybe if I lived in San Francisco instead of Dallas, I would be immersed in a sea of liberalism and the general political perspective would be different, but I live here in Big D and this is the way it is.

Left Wingers think that it is best to pay as you go. If the government spends more, then it should tax more. If the government spends less, then it should tax less. This simplistic notion is difficult to put into practice for a myriad of reasons. First, we have a huge debt, which has been accumulated by both Lefties and Righties. If one thinks that the national debt falls on one ideological group more than the other, then I think that one's perspective is too myopic. However, I am really not trying to pick apart what part of the national debt should be blamed on whom. I am trying to help (yes, help) Right Wingers understand their fellow American Left Wingers.

If any Right Winger is reading this (and there is doubt in my mind that any might be), I know they are thinking that I am out of my Left Wing mind. However, let us get real. Running a government costs money. It costs a lot of money. It really costs an unimaginable amount of money.

Instead of yelling at each other, it seems to me that we should try to figure out how to work together and negotiate federal programs that are in the best interest of our country and try to pay for them as we go. How hard is that? It is probably pretty hard given the current political landscape, but still a doable deal.

What are some (not all) of this Left Winger's ideas? First, I would do away with the current tax code and start over. I think that it is riddled with so much special interest stuff that it is unsalvageable. How would I replace it? I would do away with all tax credits, tax write offs, capital gains benefits, depreciation, tax free investments and everything which complicates the code and gives one group of people an unfair benefit over another group of people.

I would implement a flat tax. For those individuals who make less than a certain amount of money, then their tax level would graduate down. There would be no taxes on Social Security benefits.

I would prefer that each state also have a single flat rate income tax as well and that all other taxes would cease, except for sales taxes on sinful purchases. Now we may not agree on what is sinful, but I have a list of items that I think all clear thinking Americans should think are at least sinful enough to impose a sales tax: booze, weed, prostitution and other types of dope. I am not trying to encourage people to sin. In fact, I may be trying to discourage them from sinning by taxing sinful things. You know what? I have a lot of Right Wing friends who think this is a good idea, also.

If you do not know what your real federal income tax percentage is, look at your tax records. If you cannot figure it out, ask your accountant. This would be a good time to put down the book and try to figure that out.

It was reported in the Dallas Morning News on Tuesday February 3, 2009, that the wealthiest 400 Americans paid an average of 17.2% in 2006 in federal income tax. It further said that their rate had dropped from 22.9% in 2001 primarily due to the lowering of the capital gains tax to 15%. It also said that the average annual income of these top 400 was $263,300,000.00. I read (Congressional Budget Office estimate) that the family household that earns $136,400 in annual income pays 27.5% in income taxes.

I have to tell you that this rubs a Left Winger the wrong way. I will pay my taxes, not necessarily with a smile, but it is my responsibility, and I will do it. My Right Wing friends do the same. Most of us earn about the same amount of money and pay about the same amount in taxes. Here is the crux of the debate. My Right Winger friends rail against the welfare people who sit on their butts and watch Oprah and eat Fritos all day, do not work, do not pay taxes and are a drain on society. Everyone agrees that people who are physically fit and mentally capable should work and not live on the taxpayer dole. Left Wingers agree with Right Wingers! Welfare should be meted out to those who need it not those who are just too damn lazy to work. That is it. Prosecute welfare cheats.

However, and this is a big however, many people cannot work for physical or mental reasons, and they need help. Families, churches, and charitable organizations are not and have not been able to care for those people. That is why we have welfare, and why we have to pay for it with tax dollars.

One of the wealthiest people ever to run for the presidency is Mitt Romney. Except for the fact he is a moderate being forced to shout he is a born again conservative, he seems to a be good guy to me. Let's look at Mitt. He is good looking. He only has one wife (ever), he is smart, he is articulate, and he gives lots of money to charitable endeavors. His dad was an immigrant who had a great life success story. Mitt is really rich. Apparently, he made his money and did not inherit it. He earned it. Really, in many ways Mitt Romney exemplifies the American Dream. Mitt seems to follow the rules. Here is what gets my Left Wing goat with Mitt. He pays about fourteen percent on his income taxes. What do you pay working class reader, Lefty or Righty? I bet you pay a higher tax rate than Mitt.

We do have a class system in the United States of America. It is enforced by the government through the IRS. If you Right Wingers want to hear someone raise a ruckus about taxes, all you have to do is read on.

I am a second-class American. The odds are greatly in favor that you are, too. How you say? The fact is that our government creates a first class for wealthy Americans. It does it by taxing working people to the max while giving wealthy Americans tax breaks that allow them to pay fourteen percent in income taxes.

It really makes me angry when I think that my government taxes me at a higher rate than it does someone who makes a hundred or more times more money than I do. It is wrong. It is morally wrong. It defies logic. It is not right, and no one will ever convince any clear thinking person it is right.

How much harder is it for the working class to toil and try to get wealthy when they are taxed at twice (or more) the income tax rate of the rich? The answer is pretty obvious, is it not? It is almost impossible.

Why do Right Wingers pander to the extreme rich? Why do Right Wingers constantly want to give the extremely wealthy American a tax advantage that the rest of us cannot have? Why do they not believe that the rich should pay the same percentage as the middle class? This drives me crazy. I think it drives most Left Wingers crazy. (If this drives you crazy, then you may be a Left Winger and just now discovering it!)

Here is the justification that my Right Wing buddies give me. These great (rich) Americans carry our country on their backs. They are the driving force behind all which is great in America. Their financial, intellectual, political, and personal sacrifices make our country great. These are the entrepreneurs who make us the great country we are. The crescendo of this argument is this: They pay a huge percentage of the total taxes that are collected by the IRS. How much of a sacrifice should they make? These great American rich people pay a hugely disproportionate percentage of the income taxes collected, my gosh, give these great people a break. Huzzah!

Give me a break!

Let us quit whining, pay a fair flat tax, and quit pandering to the rich, the special interests, the slovenly, and whoever the heck else is receiving preferential tax treatment. That should get a big "Amen" from all straight-thinking Americans.

As ignorant as this Left Winger is about the income tax, wait till you hear my ideas on the corporate tax.

We currently have an absurdly high corporate tax in this great country of ours. The Cato Institute published that the effective U.S. Corporate Tax Rate on new investment was 34.6 percent in 2010. Further, most states have some kind of corporate tax. Ironically, there are companies not paying corporate taxes at all while others pay the high rate. Once again, this is not the way it should be.

Here we go again – flat tax. Let us put in a low, flat tax that corporations pay. It is ironic that the Right Wingers in this country call Left Wingers commies, socialists, and pinkos, because according to the Cato Institute, China has a an effective corporate tax rate of 16.6 percent and all of the European socialist countries have a lower effective corporate tax rate than the good old USA. The average effective corporate tax rate in 2010 in the 83 nations published was 17.7 percent. Does this mean that the pinkos are not as pink as we are?

I suggest that we impose a flat federal corporate tax rate of 10% and let us make all publicly traded corporations pay it. If a state wants to tax a corporation, let it impose a flat tax, too.

Surely, Left Wingers and Right Wingers can come to some way of taxing both corporations and individuals fairly. What is keeping us from getting fair taxation accomplished? I will tell you that is not Left Wingers!

Lefties and Righties call your Congressmen. We want to be taxed fairly. If your Senator or Representative, whether Democrat or Republican, votes to continue to pander to the rich, then vote that scoundrel out. Huzzah!

Crime, Drugs and Capital Punishment in America

If any of you are still reading, this may come as a surprise to you that I actually have a little first-hand knowledge of this issue. I once (long, long ago in the last century) was an assistant to the Dallas County District Attorney, Henry M. Wade.

Is the United States the most violent country in the world? I think not; yet, we have more people in prison than any other country. The U.S. Department of Justice (2008) reports 2,310,984 prisoners were held in federal or state prisons or in local jails. Prison is graduate school for criminals. The Bureau of Prisons reports that in the year 2005, the cost of keeping an inmate in a federal prison was $23,431.92 per inmate per year. The total cost of inmates would be an approximate annual cost of $54,150,977,088.00 to American taxpayers. Read that again: $54,150,977,088.00.

Why do we have so many people incarcerated? Well, there are a zillion reasons. Is there a solution to our crime issue? Maybe there is, but it will require a lot of effort. Let's face it: who cares about criminals? Our attitude is throw them in jail and throw away the keys! Anyone who thinks time in prison is not hard is nuts. Violence abounds, disease abounds, and as I mentioned earlier, one can learn an awful lot about becoming a more dangerous criminal.

I am not going to attempt to try to solve the problem of crime in our country, but I do have a few suggestions as how to reduce our prison population and perhaps reduce the crime rate as well.

The Left Winger position is that we incarcerate too many people for crimes that do not pose a danger to society. In other words, there are two kinds of criminals: those who pose a danger to society and those who do not. Those who pose a danger to society should be in prison, and those who do not should not.

Let us talk about those people who pose a danger: murderers, robbers using deadly weapons, sex offenders, and burglars. These folks need time in prison. There are other dangerous people who need time in prison: those people who import illegal drugs such as cocaine, heroin, amphetamines, and the like into our country. These are bad and dangerous people. There is another group of people who are dangerous to our society and those people are financial sociopaths. These people are dishonest to the core and will lie, cheat, steals and take money that is not theirs from anybody, and they have no remorse whatsoever. These people range from flim-flam artists to corporate thieves. These people are especially dangerous because they may seem so successful and normal while they are stealing left and right from the widows' and orphans' fund and/or people's life savings. I say to hell with them; send them to prison.

Who does not pose a threat to society? Those people who get drunk and stoned in the confines of their homes. Am I a proponent on drunkenness and "dopery"? I am certainly not (at least as far as the "dopery" goes)!

Now, this is a complicated issue. Lefties think that "dopery" and drunkenness are bad for society. I even think that Righties agree with this proposition. Both sides probably believe that the government should not be meddling in peoples' private lives as long as these people are not a danger to society. Let's forget drunkenness right now and focus on "dopery." Do not look up this word. It does not exist, but you know what it means.

I am not talking about the people who drive under the influence; I am talking about adults who go home and get wacked out. Dope is bad for them. It may kill them and cause terrible problems for their families and that is bad, bad, bad! However, it should not be illegal to be a doper.

Here is the problem with my argument. Lefties are conflicted sometimes. Where do dopers get the dope they use to whack themselves out? They get it from dope dealers. Whereas some dope dealers may be the friendly dope head next door, one does not have to go up the dope distribution chain very far before we run into dangerous scumbags who are a real threat to our society.

For some, this is the end of the story. Dope sellers are bad; therefore dopers are bad so they all need to go to prison. Fair enough, but this is not what I think most Left Wingers think is the best policy.

How do we deal with these dopers? First, I would hope that our educational system would truthfully educate children as to the problems associated with the use of dope (every kind of dope for this example). The first thing that the education process should tell these young people is that dope is bad for you and that some dope is really, really dangerous and other dope is less dangerous. Some dope is more addictive than other dope. In any case, we have to be honest and tell these kids that the reason that people do dope is because it makes them feel better. Just like alcohol, it can (and almost always will) make you feel worse, too, but it does give dopers some temporal enjoyment. The issue is the health risk/reward.

Some people really do become hooked on some types of dope from the first usage, and their lives dramatically become worse. Others use the same dope and continue to use it periodically and apparently live normal lives. I do not know the statistics, but I have seen it go both ways.

The real truth is that alcohol is a type of drug that we believe (I certainly do) is socially acceptable. We believe this even though alcohol causes more problems than all types of dope combined (once again my opinion).

Marijuana also is bad for you, but is it any worse than alcohol? Maybe yes, maybe no. That is not the point. The point is that people who are users have no business being in prison. If they drive under the influence and hurt someone, it is a different story.

People are growing marijuana all over the place. People are smoking it everywhere. The criminalization of marijuana is a joke. Legalize it and tax it like we do tobacco (another problem substance but not for this chapter)!

Hooray, did we solve that problem? I have to tell you that a lot of my Right Winger and Left Winger friends smoke marijuana. Legalize it, tax it, regulate it, and get on with it.

Unfortunately, marijuana is a unique situation. I am talking about the legalization (only softies call it decriminalization) of just about all types of dope. Some are more terrible for the dopers than others.

This may not be a Left-Right issue, but generally Lefties are more in tune with this type of thinking than Righties.

Once again, DOPE IS BAD! I say do not use DOPE! Dope may ruin your life. It may ruin your family. It may kill you, and it may kill your friends. It causes many more problems than it solves. Does it really solve any problems?

How do we legalize dope? Would the legalization of dope actually make our crime rate go down, or would it lead to a country of drugged out zombies?

Dope is made all over the place both in the USA and in other countries. It is almost never made under strict laboratory conditions. Yet, dopers put it into their bodies as if the FDA had approved it as safe for every dope use imaginable. This is a real problem. I want dopers to know that dope is not only bad; it is nasty and may be contaminated. There are all sorts of ways dope is bad for you and might kill you, but that is not what I am talking about here. I am talking about the legalization of dope.

This must really sound crazy to any of you Righties who have stuck it out so far, but I think the legalization in the big picture is better than our current policy of interdiction has been or will ever be.

I think that we have learned that there are literally millions of Americans who use dope illegally and will continue to do so who are otherwise law abiding citizens. These are not violent or dangerous people. (Here again, I am not talking about wackos who break all kinds of laws to get money for dope.) Sure you can argue that an axe murderer might pay his taxes and otherwise be a good citizen, but that is a little absurd, don't you think?

These semi law abiding dopers are breaking the law and risking their entire careers and freedom just to get doped up. While that seems nuts to me, it is what it is. The illegality of dope for these dopers instills a sense of devaluation of law-abidingness. This is really bad for our society.

In case you think I am on dope right now for these opinions, I want to emphasize that I hate dope. I hate what dope does to our society. I hate that many of my friend's children have been wrecked by dope. If there is anything you get from this chapter it is this: "Do not use dope!"

Having said all of that, what percentage of the people in prison or jail in the United States today are locked up primarily because they are dope addicts? Let us assume that 25% of all incarcerated people are in for drug possession and or possession with intent to deliver (usually to an undercover police officer) or distribution, which is usually selling a small amount of drugs to a police officer. The cost of incarceration for these people would be 25% of the cost of our total prison expenditures which would mean that the tax payers would save $13,500,000,000 per year (thirteen billion five hundred million dollars). If we legalized dope and freed those being incarcerated for it, we would free approximately 575,000 people who are in prison primarily for drug offenses (these are my estimates).

So what are the other costs of interdiction for drug offenses? Police manpower could be reassigned and operated more efficiently. Court expenses would fall. While it may seem ludicrous to many, we might see some of these people actually working and paying taxes. While they are in jail, who is supporting their families? Take a wild guess. You and I are paying taxes to support the children of these jail birds with what we call welfare! It is a vicious economic cycle.

Having pontificated about the legalization of drugs, I want to reemphasize that I think using drugs is bad. Do not use drugs.

We have another issue in the criminal law arena that bears some discussion: capital punishment. Is capital punishment a good idea? When I was in law school studying criminal law, we were taught that the punishment should fit the crime. The main factors we should consider were deterrence, rehabilitation, and retribution. There are lots of other factors, but these were the big three that we studied.

In the case of capital punishment, I do not think that the deterrent factor makes much difference to a cold blooded killer. Are we really trying to rehabilitate a person sentenced to death?

What about retribution? What do we mean when we talk about retribution? This is harm for harm or eye-for-eye punishment. People (and I suppose lots of people including some of the families of victims) do get a sense of satisfaction when a convicted murderer gets executed. I understand that.

Is capital punishment worth it to society? I am discussing the satisfaction some get from the execution of the sentence and the financial cost of the capital murder trial and appeal. I do not want to bore you with statistics on this issue, but it is actually cheaper to house a convicted murderer for 40 years than it is to pay for the trial, the appeal, the housing during the process, and the execution. In fact, the cost is about three times as expensive for the execution of an inmate as opposed to keeping that inmate in prison for 40 years. According to the Death Penalty Information Center, it costs Texas about $2,300,000 to implement a capital punishment case from arrest to execution. That is a lot of money to execute one person.

Is it worth it? Is it worth $2,300,000 to prosecute someone and achieve an execution? How do economic conservatives feel about this? How do liberals feel about this? Does capital punishment make us safer? Does capital punishment give us any real benefit other than the sense of relief that a convicted murderer has been executed? Is that worth $2,300,000?

Who makes the decision as to whom to prosecute for a capital offense? The prosecutor usually has the discretion to decide whether to negotiate a plea bargain, try the case as a murder (non-capital offense), or a capital murder offense.

Is the elimination of capital punishment something that we as a society should consider? I am not talking about the capture of terrorists or enemy combatants in war. I am discussing whether society really benefits from capital punishment for those convicted of murder. I say it does not.

As a former prosecutor, I believe that it is certainly possible for an innocent person to be found guilty and sentenced to death. As great as our legal system is, mistakes are made. As horrible a mistake as the execution of an innocent person could be; that is not why I have changed my mind on the issue.

Why am I against the death penalty when there are plenty of Lefties who are pro death penalty? There are two main reasons, and neither is constitutional.

First, I think that the death penalty is not a deterrent to crime. While it certainly deters the person who is executed from committing any more crimes, I do not think that a killer generally thinks that he or she should not kill someone because he or she might get the death penalty. A few murderers might think this way but not enough to affect my thinking. I would be amazed that some potential murderer would decide to be peaceful because of the deterring affect of the death penalty. Therefore, in my mind the only justification for it is retribution. For this Left Winger, retribution alone is not a good enough justification for the death penalty.

Second, it is an extremely inefficient and costly use of tax dollars. Look up the statistics; I am not making this up. It is much more expensive to prosecute a death penalty case than to sentence an individual for life in prison. It does not seem possible, but there are so many things that appear one way but in reality are another. The Dallas Morning News also reported that it costs approximately $2,300,000 to prosecute a death penalty case, which is about three times the cost of prosecuting a person for life in prison. How much taxpayer money is being spent? There are approximately 3,200 inmates on death row in the United States according to the Death Penalty Focus. What is the cost for these 3,200 death penalty cases over the course of the prosecution? The answer is $7,360,000,000. That is right. Over seven billion tax dollars and climbing. If we no longer prosecuted these killers for life in prison, we would save about $5,000,000,000. This is not an annual savings. This is the savings over the course of an entire death penalty case: investigation to actual execution which takes years and years. Still $5,000,000,000 is a lot of money. I do not think it is a reasonable expenditure of tax payers' dollars.

When I consider my second objection to the death penalty along with my first objection, it just does not make sense to have it any more. I would think that my Right Wing friends would oppose the death penalty on financial reasons alone. My friend, E. X. Martin III, a great and well known criminal attorney, and no supporter of the Right Wing, asked me how Republicans could cope with the dilemma of capital punishment. I was not as swift as E. X. and I asked, "What dilemma?" He said that one of the biggest cost factors in the prosecution of capital cases is attorneys fees. He went on to say that capital punishment could not be worth it to the Right Wing if they understood it helped attorneys. Who knows, if enough Right Wingers read this book, we may do away with capital punishment in this country.

Do we really not see the benefit to the legalization of drugs and the elimination of the death penalty? Would our society erode? I do not think so. Would we have a more sensible legal system? I think so. Would we save billions of dollars? We absolutely would. Would we be able to raise billions of tax dollars? You better believe we would.

As time passes, more and more of my Right Wing friends are beginning to agree with me. Perhaps they are not agreeing because they are becoming more liberal. Perhaps it is because they are thinking about these issues and realizing that it is so sensible to make these changes.

Honestly, we can and should have the best criminal justice system in the world. This requires constant thought, effort, and an understanding that things do change, and the justice system must also change. We currently have too many people in prison who do not need to be there. This is an undue burden to our taxpayers. It can and should be better, and I think these changes will make it better. It is not a Left Wing or Right Wing argument. It is or at least should be an evolution to improve our justice system.

The Constitution of the United States of America

So many scholars have written so much about this document, I am almost embarrassed to write anything as I am sure I cannot add anything meaningful to the overall discussion. Despite that and as a loyal Left Winger, I will charge into the fray!

I try to read the Constitution once a year. I was an American History major in college, where the Constitution looms large. I first really began to appreciate it there. I remember we studied civics in high school, but to tell you the truth that was so long ago, I do not remember anything about it.

When I went to law school, Constitutional Law was one of my favorite courses. I always thought how cool it would be to be able to say I was a Constitutional Law expert. Trust me, I am not saying that at all. I have read it many times, and I may understand it more than the next person, but I am no expert in Constitutional Law.

Everyone knows that the United States Constitution is the fundamental law of the land, and that any law that is passed by either Congress or any Legislature in any state must pass muster in its Constitutionality or it will eventually be voided by the Supreme Court of the United States of America. That is not the part of the Constitution which I want to focus on.

I want to talk about the Bill of Rights.

We have all heard this phrase, but many of us do not know what it is exactly or why it exists. I will attempt to discuss both very quickly and then, hopefully, discuss what this Left Winger thinks about the state of our rights in this great country now.

What is the Bill of Rights? It is the name given to the first ten amendments to the United States Constitution. What these amendments do is restrict the power of government. They are important. They are really important. They are perhaps the most important laws we have.

Today, the Bill of Rights is not as powerful as it once was, and that is a tragedy. Our Founding Fathers understood the importance of restricting the power of the government. It seems that very few of us do today, and it is a shame.

Why has the Bill of Rights been eroded? I am sure that there are many reasons. Here are just a few. First, our freedoms today are taken for granted. Only a tiny portion of our population has ever lived under real tyranny. Our Founding Fathers understood the power of the king (central government), and they wanted to harness it. Since then, we have had generations of Americans living in this great and free country and fewer and fewer people appreciate the importance of keeping a check on the powers of the federal government. Lord Acton's wise saying, "Power corrupts and absolute power corrupts absolutely," often falls on deaf ears.

All lovers of our Constitution have favorite clauses and amendments. Here are mine. Amendment One: "Congress shall make no law respecting an establishment of religion, or prohibiting the free exercise thereof; or abridging the freedom of speech, or of the press; or the right of the people to peaceably assemble, and to petition the government for a redress of grievances." That, my friends, is beautiful. It is the font of freedom: freedom of speech, freedom of religion and freedom of the press. These are the fundamental freedoms that make our country great. Lefties agree, Righties agree, hallelujah!

Here is a potential shock for all of you brave souls who are still reading this: I own three pistols. If you break into my house at night, I am going to shoot you dead. Wow! A Lefty who owns a gun; say it ain't so. I am not a Second Amendment nut, but it is a fundamental right in this country. Here is another gem for you Righties: a lot of Lefties own guns. I also have a very low regard for a burglar who would break into my house at night.

Amendment Four: "The right of the people to be secure in their persons, houses, papers, and effects, against unreasonable searches and seizures, shall not be violated, and no warrants shall issue, but upon probable cause, supported by oath or affirmation, and particularly describing the place to be searched, and the persons or things to be seized." This is fundamental. This is important and this right has been eroded to the point that it is almost a joke. It has been eroded for many reasons. Unfortunately, it has been eroded to help the police fight crime, and I will assert mainly to help police fight drug crime. Folks, the Fourth Amendment is not a technicality; it is a basic and fundamentally important right. I regret how our courts have eroded its power.

Amendment Five: "No person shall be held to answer for a capital, or otherwise infamous crime, unless on a presentment or indictment of a grand jury, except in cases arising in the land or naval forces, or in the militia, when in actual service in time of war or public danger; nor shall any person be subject for the same offense to be twice put in jeopardy of life or limb;

nor shall be compelled in any criminal case to be a witness against himself, nor be deprived of life, liberty, or property, without due process of law; nor shall private property be taken for public use without just compensation." This is a powerful and broad amendment. Unfortunately, the courts continue to erode its power. The loss of these rights really makes me sick at my stomach. What has been lost? The idea of a prohibition against double jeopardy has long been gone. If the state prosecutor cannot convict a person, the federal prosecutor can use a federal statute and come right back on that person. Same facts but the courts have said this is not double jeopardy. What a joke! It is double jeopardy, and it is un-American. I defy anyone to argue against me on this issue.

Amendment Six: "In all criminal prosecutions, the accused shall enjoy the right to a speedy and public trial, by an impartial jury of the State and district wherein the crime shall have been committed, which district shall have been previously ascertained by law, and to be informed of the nature and cause of the accusation; to be confronted with the witnesses against him; to have compulsory process for obtaining witnesses in his favor, and to have the assistance of counsel for his defense." How many of you recall this famous quote, "The first thing we must do is kill all the lawyers." It is from Shakespeare's Henry VI. It is one of the most misunderstood quotations of all time. It is routinely spouted at cocktail parties, political parties, political speeches, you name it. It is a reference to the idea held by many that lawyers are a hindrance to someone's freedom or way of life.

What did Shakespeare mean when he penned this famous (shall I say infamous) quotation? The statement was made by none other than Dick the Butcher. It meant that in order for chaos and evil to prevail, let us remove those who will protect truth, order, and society: lawyers!

Yes, I am a lawyer. I believe that the field of law is the most important and cherished profession we have in this great country. Yes, there are crooked lawyers. But, we as the lawyers in this great country protect YOUR fundamental rights! I like a lawyer joke as much as the next person. What I find undermining to our entire system of rights and freedoms is the general disdain for the legal profession. Why is that? Sure, we have bad lawyers, but is that the real reason that lawyers are held in low public esteem? Nope, it is not.

Left Wingers appreciate that we have lawyers that stand up and protect our rights. Left Wingers understand that it is often only his or her lawyer that keeps a wrongly accused individual from prison. Left Wingers know that it is lawyers who keep the rich and powerful from usurping the rights of the weak and underrepresented. Who is it that gripes about lawyers? You guessed it: Right Wingers.

Here is my experience in the field of Personal Injury Law. When Left Wingers get hurt and come into my office to discuss representation, they want to know what the law is and if there is a case where I can recover money for their losses. When Right Wingers get hurt and come into my office, they want to tell me that they are not like "those people" and are really hurt and despite not believing in hiring a personal injury lawyer, they are going to do it anyway. I kindly respond that they are exactly like "those people," and I will represent them like I do all injured people. We are all the same. Somehow, Right Wingers are convinced that seeking compensation for their injuries is morally wrong until they get hurt. Then they try to believe that they are somehow different than other injured people. We are all the same. The only difference is that Right Wingers have been deluded into thinking that they are different than the rest of us.

The Fifth Amendment underscores our Founding Father's understanding that lawyers protect the basic rights, values and laws which we hold dear. It makes my heart swell to be an attorney, and I am not kidding!

As a fine Lefty, I have to at least mention Amendment Eight: "Excessive bail shall not be required, nor excessive fines imposed, nor cruel and unusual punishment inflicted." I used to be ambivalent about the death penalty. I knew most Lefties are agin' it, but I was ambivalent. I like to think that Left Wingers are a group of intellectually and clear thinking people who do not think in lock step on every issue (probably the same thing can be said about Righties). I do think that we have too many laws and that to incarcerate anyone for dope is cruel and unusual.

I am now against the death penalty. Is it cruel and unusual? It is cruel. Killing someone, even under the authority of the government, is cruel. Is it unusual? I guess that depends on what one might call unusual. Since it does not happen frequently, I will go ahead and say that it is unusual. That is not my real objection, however. I understand that many believe that the death penalty is unconstitutional because it is cruel and unusual. I say it is not practical.

There it is. As I said, I am no expert on Constitutional Law, although it is a cool expression. However, I do feel pretty strongly about the importance of our Bill of Rights and the importance of keeping a check on the power of the government.

After you finish reading this book, go read the Constitution of the United States of America. You will feel really good about yourself (as opposed to how you may feel now). It is what separates America from everybody else.

Race Relations

If talking about politics and religion is not enough to get you agitated, surely a discussion of racial relations will.

In this Left Winger's opinion, anyone who dismisses racial conflict as a thing of the past is not seeing reality. Race is an important and potentially inflammatory issue in this country. I think it is worth talking about.

Is there even one Left Winger in this country who thinks that African-Americans (dark skinned toned people with African heritage) have the same opportunity that white Americans have? I doubt it. Oddly enough, a huge percentage of Right Wingers strongly disagree.

Why is that? It is a long and wretched story.

What can be done about the issue seems more productive to me than how we got into this condition.

No matter how much everyone may want race relations to improve, it is not going to happen just because this Left Winger has a good idea or two.

There is no doubt in my mind that the great equalizer for the long haul is good and available public education for everyone. Better education provides better jobs, better lives, and better opportunity. It will not solve every problem, but it will solve a lot of them.

As an aside, if we were to walk onto one of Dallas' finest country clubs, what would we notice? I can tell you right now. We would see very few black members. Is that because everyone in these clubs is a member of the Ku Klux Klan? No, that is not the reason. I doubt that there are any Klansmen in any country clubs in Dallas. Are there racists? Sure there are, at least some. That is not the real reason you do not see a slew of black members, however. The real reason is that there are so few (relatively speaking) rich black people who want to spend a ton of money joining a golf club. However, if the percentage of wealthy black people were the same as the percentage of wealthy white people, you would see a heck of a lot more black members in country clubs. Imagine, if Tiger Woods lived in Dallas, these country clubs would be clamoring for his membership! They would also clamor for Justice Clarence Thomas! They might even clamor for a well-known black (maybe Republican) athlete named Charles Barkley! What these country clubs are not clamoring for is poor people of any race.

Money makes more of a determining factor than race when it comes to country club membership. Not that most of us give a flip about being a member of a country club, but it is illustrative of the difficulties that black people have in our society.

While that sounds so simple and so easy, it is a monumental proposition. I live in Dallas, Texas. We seem to have a jillion private schools. Why do we have so many? (By the way, the term a jillion means a whole lot.) I believe that for one reason or another, many Dallasites think that a private education is superior to a public education for their children. That is almost certainly and, unfortunately, true.

Ironically, one of the best public school systems in the United States is right smack dab in the middle of Dallas: the Highland Park Independent School District.

Do not confuse the Highland Park Independent School District with the Dallas Independent School District. They are very different. Although it is not true that everyone who lives within the Highland Park Independent School District is rich, it is certainly a very wealthy school district.

What makes Highland Park so successful? There are a lot of reasons. Let us click off a few. The schools are in a wealthy and safe part of town. Teachers feel safe there. The parents are not only generally wealthy, they are well educated. They can pay for tutors. Many families have only one parent who works. It has a history of academic excellence.

Safety, unfortunately, is a big factor in where many good teachers go to teach. It is shocking to me that so many schools are located in areas where teachers are worried about their safety. Teachers take less money to teach at Highland Park. If a campus is not safe, it will be hard to attract the best teachers. Creating a safe environment is not something that a school district can do by itself. It needs help from the community. It needs volunteers.

Highland Park gets parent volunteers by the drove. How is that possible? Wealthy people tend to have only one parent working. The care-giver parent volunteers at Highland Park schools. Also, well educated people not only understand the value of an education, they know how to help in the educational process because they are educated. These people feel comfortable in and around schools because they are educated. Also, there is very little doubt that educated parents have the skills to help their children more academically than uneducated parents.

Does this mean that the Dallas Independent School District and other large underperforming school districts are doomed because of the dearth of wealthy and educated parents within the district? No, but it means that a whole lot of work needs to be done.

Let me focus on the Dallas Independent School District. There are lots of families who do not have either wealthy or educated parents. However, there are a lot of parents who could and I am sure would volunteer if the right opportunity presented itself. Additionally, there are a lot of wealthy and educated parents within the school district.

What if the District were to create an office of District Volunteerism where the District determined what and who was needed where. This office and its volunteer staff could advertise over the Internet and through the media asking people from all walks of life to volunteer some of their valuable free time to improve the quality of public education in the district.

There would be openings for almost everyone who was willing to volunteer. Non-educated people to Ph.D.s could come through the volunteer office and go where they could be best utilized. As I have mentioned, I am an attorney. Surprisingly, there is abundant talent available from the attorneys in this city willing to volunteer. These are educated people. Maybe if enough volunteers signed up, the time commitment might be only an hour or two per week.

How can volunteers make a campus safer? I guarantee that if you have enough neighborhood volunteers on campus, picking up trash, keeping their eyes open, and reporting suspicious behavior, it would have a huge effect on the safety of campuses. These people need not have degrees. They just need to be dedicated to the proposition that each of their contributions is helping just a little bit, and with enough help, the problem begins to disappear. I think it could and would work.

People can help all over the school system doing everything from picking up trash to minor maintenance. People can be teacher assistants. They can be mentors. It could and would work. It will take a lot of effort, but I believe in my Lefty mind that it would work.

Is the effort worth it? How valuable is a high quality public education? How much can this help improve minority classrooms all over the country? I think a lot.

If enough Americans put their hearts, their minds, and their bodies into solving a problem, it will get solved. Does that cure race relations? No, it does not. However, it starts to give minority students the ability to have an equal footing with their wealthy white counterparts.

Is education the only remedy to racial disparity in this country. Heck no, it is certainly not. There are a zillion problems, and where there is a problem, there is a solution. So I would say there are about a zillion things that can be done to improve race relations. I am only discussing a few solutions.

Lefties tend to focus on the inequities brought about by white people against black people. Believe it or not, I know that these are not the in vogue terms describing racial distinctions, but I never understood how they are really racially insensitive. After all, white people are not white and black people are not black. If this is a big issue for you, then I think you are too sensitive.

I am getting off point here. What I want to do is talk briefly on what I would call the issue of black awareness. Get ready, this may be a mistake!

When I was a child, my mother told me that I could do anything I wanted to do. If I wanted to, I could be the President of the United States! When I was young, I believed it. As I got older, I realized there were a lot of things I could not do because I did not have enough talent. For instance, I was never going to be a great rock and roll piano player. However, there was nothing I thought I could not do just because I am white.

I do not believe that black people told their children that they could do anything they wanted to do because they believed it was a lie. They thought or knew that simply by being black there were social barriers which could not be broken.

Black parents were not telling their children that when they grew up they could be President of the United States. I think that black people (and white people) thought that hell would freeze over before a black man would get elected President.

Well, I'll be darned.

Does the election of Barack Obama end racial differences in this country? No, but I tell you, in this Left Winger's opinion, it is a huge step in the right direction. I mean huge. Now, everyone on the planet knows that a black man can be elected President of the United States of America. What does that say? It says that racial equality is moving forward in our great country.

Now black parents need to realize how empowering this is. Seize the moment! Assert the importance of the American Dream to your children. It is a reality.

In 2004, I thought the chances of a black American getting elected President of the United States was less than a cow jumping over the moon. I am thrilled to say how wrong I was. If you have had feelings of persecution or whatever, try to put them behind you. This is a new beginning. We have had beginnings before, but not like this one!

Most Left Wingers would not talk about this, but I am not part of the herd, I guess. I agree with Bill Cosby, Barack Obama, and others. Black Americans have to figure out how to solve some of the problems that plague their community. I am mainly talking about problems with the breakdown of the family. I can tell everyone that will listen, or in this case read, but it really does not make much difference. I can talk about it. I can write about it. I can complain about it, but I cannot make it go away. I think education is huge. I think church is huge. I think political empowerment is huge. However, all of these are not enough. We need more black (and every other kind) leaders to come forward and accept more self responsibility. All of us have a huge responsibility to our families. That is it. We need to try everything we can to make it work.

Unfortunately, I have to say that education, hard work, and volunteerism does not make racism go away. It helps, but it does not make it disappear. Today's racism is much more subtle than it has been in the past. In fact, I believe that most white people are not aware of how subtle racism even operates.

This is ugly. Has any President before Barack Obama been harassed about his birth certificate? Oddly enough, John McCain was born in Panama; yet I never heard one person ask him to present his birth certificate. What about Barry Goldwater? He was not born in a state. He was born in Arizona before it became a state. How about George Romney, Mitt's father?

He was born in Mexico. Were people asking about his birth certificate?

What is different about Barack Obama from these other men? One can argue (I might add in a most specious way) Barack Obama's father was a Kenyan. None of the other candidates' fathers was not an American. There is another more obvious reason and you know what it is: subtle racism.

Was this tactic effective? Did it make people go crazy? Did it make people think that the Democrats, liberals, and Barack Obama were involved in the world's greatest conspiracy to elect a non-American to the Presidency; to somehow turn our country into some God-knows-what? Yes, it was effective. While the overwhelming majority of intellectual Republicans now have no doubt that Barack Obama was born August 4, 1961 in Honolulu, Hawaii, there are still some holdouts that have been so indoctrinated that they still think he is not an American.

Indoctrinated with subtle racism.

Subtle racism is a very powerful tool. I do not want anyone to think that only white Right Wingers are affected by subtle racism. All of us are subject to being influenced by this insidious instrument of wickedness. Until all people clear their hearts, and I mean all people, racism will be alive and well. However, I do believe we are making huge progress in race relations despite those mean-spirited people who manipulate us with all types of subtle racism.

Let us work together. Let us concentrate on positive action. Let us quit fussing at each other. Let us recognize and celebrate our cultural and racial differences and not battle over our differences. I have to tell you I get so sick of hearing how one race is so much better than the other race in this or that. Does it really matter? Should a child in this country not be encouraged to play golf because of his color? Should a child in this country not be encouraged to play basketball because of his color? Should anyone be discouraged from doing anything that his or her skills, intelligence, and hard work will not allow? We intellectualize this; now let us all implement it.

Do not think that I believe that reading this book will make everyone run outside, hold hands, sing Kum Ba Yah, and our troubles will be over. They will not, although it is a great song. However, I do think that race relations will not improve unless we work together to help each other out. We are a multicultural and multiracial country. Why do we not celebrate our cultural strengths and differences? Let us learn more about each other. Let us try to be positive. Let us make the kind of progress that we all believe is possible in this great country.

It is so ironic to me that our Founding Fathers, who established this great country and wrote such brilliant, moving, and beautiful statements about our country, including my favorite, "We hold these truths to be self-evident, that *all men are created equal,* that they are endowed by their Creator with certain unalienable Rights, that among these are *Life, Liberty and the pursuit of Happiness,"* did not really believe it.

Unfortunately, they did not believe that all men are created equal. If they had, they surely would have abolished slavery. We can revise history all we want to, but the fact remains that most of our Founding Fathers were racists. I assure you that is not how most white Americans characterize them. I fall into this group. I talk about how brilliant, brave, charismatic, committed to Democracy, and eloquent they were. What I have to accept is that we also need to add racist.

Does the racism of our Founding Fathers affect us today? I am not sure. I am sure that racism exists, and it is an evil thing. It affects almost all of us; red, yellow, black, and white. Dealing with it requires a great amount of soul searching and self awareness.

If any of us find ourselves in a conversation where we are disparaging of people of different races, think about what is going on. Be on your guard about these things. If your children are listening to you or your friends belittle people of different races, they will accept that type of thought process as acceptable and normal. That is how subtle racism exists. This is an important point. I am not pointing at any political or ideological group. All of us are susceptible to this problem. I am just asking all of us to be aware of this problem.

O.K., I have called our Founding Fathers racists. However, I do believe that we cherish those words now more than ever and that we do believe more than ever that "All men and women are created equal by their creator." I know I do, and I really believe the overwhelming majority of Americans do, too.

Feminism

What is Feminism? Why do almost all Left Wingers think it is a good thing and so many Right Wingers think it is a bad thing?

I looked it up. Feminism is defined as the doctrine advocating social, political and all other rights of women equaling those of men and/or an organized movement for the attainment of such rights for women. I have to get this off my chest. *How could anyone think this concept is bad? Who in the United States of America thinks women should not have the same rights as men?*

I would like to review a little personal background. My father was killed when I was six years old. My mother was thirty-three years old, and she had no job and two boys. I was six and my brother was almost two. My maternal grandmother lived in Austin near our home. My paternal grandmother lived in Eunice, Louisiana.

Mother had to get busy. Her story is very compelling and really a lot more interesting than this book for sure! Anyway, I was raised by a single mother who happened to go back to college get a Masters and a Ph. D. You talk about a Left Winger, Whoooeeeee! There you have it. An acorn does not fall far from the tree.

I have a theory about why my Right Winger friends are against feminism, and it goes like this: God is a conservative and manly God. God wants men to run the show. God wants women to stay home and submit to their husbands (take a look at Ephesians 5:22-24). If anything runs contrary to that, then it is wrong, wrong, wrong!

For those of you Right Wingers who have other issues with Feminism and want to express those opinions, write a nasty review of this chapter.

Somebody ought to look up the meaning of the Greek word for *submit* in Ephesians. Does it really mean submit? Do your own research. A little Biblical study cannot hurt anyone. Do we live in a country where half of the people should not have equal rights with the other half? How can somebody honestly think that is a good idea? Are we so dogmatic that we really believe that women are inferior to men and that women should not have equal rights or opportunities as men do because of some Biblical interpretation?

I am not going to mention any names, but recently, a very popular (at least among Right Wingers) radio personality called a young woman a slut and a prostitute. He did this, presumably, because he did not support her political views.

I am a peace-loving guy. I have two daughters, whom I love. Their mother and I have tried to raise them to be good Christian citizens, who have their own views about life and politics. They were raised to be confident and to express their views whenever they believe it is appropriate. I want the best for my daughters. Honestly, I want the best for everyone's children.

The commentator's rant against this young woman is awful. It is reprehensible. It is outrageous. It is indefensible. It reveals something about this man. It is ugly. It is anti-woman. It is way more than anti-feminism. Anyone, and I mean anyone, who defends his comments should seriously consider getting psychiatric care. If he had called one of my daughters a slut and a prostitute, I would have to use every fiber of my conscious and civilized Left Wing being not to confront him and to whip his ass.

Now that I am slightly calmer, I wonder how it is that people in the twenty-first century can object to equality among the sexes. Are there people who really think that a man should be paid more for the exact same job as a woman doing the same exact job? Do these people think that (God forbid) if a woman were elected to be the President of the United States, that she should be paid less than a male President? Should a man be paid more for being a teacher, a coach, a police officer, or whatever? That is the way it is.

In today's difficult economic times, should a woman not be able to work outside the home? What if she is a divorcee or a widow? Should not every woman be able to have every right that a man has? What is up with that? Feminists are those people, and I am one, who supports female equality.

Left Wingers are all feminists. We are not afraid that women will take away our manly jobs. We believe that all of us can share the workplace, and we should all be treated equally under the law. I am astonished that anyone could not be pro feminism.

Homosexuality

What is it about being a homosexual that makes so many of us feel awkward? Are the majority of us, even Left Wingers, at least a little homophobic?

Am I homophobic? I really do not think I am. Perhaps you will agree with me after you read this chapter. Perhaps you will disagree and perhaps you will not care what I am at all. I have to interject that by this time in most books I read I do not care what the author's opinion is. You may feel the same way I do.

Does it matter if I am or am not a homophobe? I think probably not. Does it matter if you are a homophobe? You think about it.

What I do want to focus on is what I think a principal of Left Wingerism is; treating people with respect and equality in the law. I am not asking anybody to embrace homosexuality or to try out homosexual behavior. I am urging each of us to live by the Golden Rule.

I have previously mentioned that I am a Presbyterian. The members of our church are probably similar to most large Protestant churches in the United States today. Good people trying to do the right thing. We spend a lot of time trying to figure out how the Church should relate to gay people. It is a mess.

Should we allow homosexuals in the ministry? Should homosexuals be allowed to marry? Should homosexuality be considered normal (whatever that means)? The list goes on and on.

I am not trying to make the issue of homosexuality a religious issue. As a matter of fact, I want to avoid that pitfall as much as I can, except to emphasize that a lot of Protestants think that homosexuality is not just a sin, but it is about the biggest sin they can imagine.

I just cannot help myself. I have to talk about Protestant churches, not all of them, but I will bet the majority of them. There are references in the Bible that include homosexual behavior as sinful. There is no doubt about that.

Here is the point which irks me. Let us assume, and I am not taking this position, but let us assume that homosexual behavior is sinful. Now let us try to figure out who among us is not a sinner of one kind or another. Spend some time thinking about it. If you are not a sinner, then you probably will not appreciate what I have to say.

Lots of people believe that sin is sin, and everyone is a sinner and that no one is perfect. These people would think that all sin is equal, at least in the eyes of the Lord. Since none of us is perfect, we have to deal with our sins or imperfections or issues or whatever it is that we have to work out. Now, whether a gay person has any issues over being gay or not is not really my point, because I am really talking about a heterosexual Left Winger's thinking and not a homosexual Left Winger's thinking.

Other people must think that homosexuality is the worst possible problem facing the world because of the attitudes that they manifest toward gay people.

I do want to say that this is not necessarily a Left Wing versus Right Wing issue. It is just an issue, and I am going to discuss it from my Left Winger perspective.

When I was a kid, I remember the big issues from the pulpit being lack of tithing, greed, adultery, coveting, idol worship, hatred, lack of faith, dishonesty, you know, the old stuff. I am sure that there were other issues, like Godless Communism, swearing, and gluttony; I just cannot remember them all. Anyway, I never remember hearing the word homosexuality coming from the pulpit as a child. And believe me, I was at church every Sunday (usually twice).

Today, what I hear is how the homosexuals and other liberal people are going to ruin the world. It seems that homosexuals and liberals are always thrown together. Have you ever heard that homosexuals and conservatives were going to ruin the world? How difficult is it for a gay person to hold conservative beliefs? I do not know. I do know that many of my conservative friends are generally not gay friendly. Anyway, what I hear from the pulpit is sinful homosexuality this, and sinful homosexuality that; those pesky homosexuals want to be considered normal, and they want to be preachers and on and on and on and on and on. My gosh, one would think that all other forms of sinful behavior have been conquered, the only sin left is homosexuality, and it is the greatest problem ever in the history of Christendom!

There I said it! (Actually, I wrote it, but I say it, too!)

Now, let us think about it. Do we really think homosexuality is the worst thing in the world? Even if you hate homosexuality, do you really believe it is the worst problem in the world?

I have a theory. The great question is why do preachers focus on the sin of homosexuality so darn much? Is it really because it is the worst behavior in the history of the human race or is there a more subtle, practical and wily reason?

As I sit in my congregation, I look around, and I see a slew of sinners just like myself. The overwhelming majority of us are not homosexuals because our church does not make homosexuals feel welcome. We have all sorts of sinners. I would like to list some for you so that you can compare my list with the list of sin and sinners at your church. Let us start off with the "Seven Deadly Sins." I did not grow up Catholic but I like this list: Pride, Covetousness, Lust, Anger, Gluttony, Envy, and Sloth. That is a good start. It does not cover bearing false witness or as we say "lyin." It does not cover murder. It does not cover a lot of really famous sins, but let us just leave it at this.

Jimmy Carter was roundly thought of as some sort of a nut by the press (the liberal press?) when he said he had lust in his heart. Apparently, the press was not familiar with Mathew 5:28. Maybe you are not either. If not, stop here, go get a Bible, and read it. Heck, just read the entire fifth chapter of Matthew. You will learn more from that than you will from one thousand political books. After you have read the fifth chapter of Matthew, I hope you will return to my book.

So why are these preachers preaching about homosexuality when there are so many other important sins out there to hammer on? Here is the secret. These congregations are full of all kinds of sinners, and these congregants have all kinds of sin. But remember who is not made welcome in these churches? Homosexuals are not made to feel welcome, so there are not a lot of homosexuals in the congregation! Therefore, these preachers know they can preach about how bad homosexualism is to the congregation because the preacher will not offend any of them! The preacher is not likely to cause some big givers to quit giving because he has emphasized the evil nature of being a homosexual. In fact, he has inflamed the congregation by preying on their latent or blatant homophobia. This is the message: "Give to the Lord, or we will be overrun by homosexuals!" When the congregation hears this message, they get those checkbooks out.

Can you imagine preaching about adultery? The preacher might offend about half the congregation. What about preaching about greed? Goodness, the preacher would offend about 90% of the congregation. What about bearing false witness (cheating on one's income taxes)? This kind of preaching is what is now called "meddlin." How can a preacher get the congregation to dig down and tithe if he is going to criticize his congregation and make them feel like sinners? The simple answer is to find a whipping sin. The whipping sin is homosexuality.

If I were a preacher, and I realize that this concept is practically blasphemous, I would take a completely different (but equally disingenuous) tact. I would preach each week about one of every kind of sin I could think of and challenge those who do not suffer from that particular sin of the week to get out the check book and write a check to help those other people who sin so much. I know human nature. Every week everyone in the congregation would be thinking that they better write a check or the person sitting next to him or her might think that he or she is a adulterer or a murderer or a liar or a coveter. I would not preach the same old let's whip the homosexuals sermon. I could raise a ton of money!

I would be embarrassed if I were a preacher whose preaching style was to fear monger the congregation about the so called great sin of homosexuality.

I am so glad to have written that. However, that is not really what the crux of this chapter is really about. What I really want to talk about is how I, as a big talking Left Winger, feel about some homosexual issues.

Should homosexuals be allowed to be preachers in mainstream protestant churches? Are you kidding? Yes, they should. If you have a standard of only hiring preachers who do not sin, then you have a pretty small group of preachers (NONE).

A liberal friend of mine pointed out to me that these preachers that I have just called out can separate the sin of homosexuality from all these other sins because homosexuals are not asking forgiveness for the sin of homosexuality or asking to be cleansed from this sin. My response is, really? Are these preachers telling us that all the aforementioned sins and the sinners who posses these sins are really repentant? Do these preachers really believe this? Heck, if that were the case, then in short order, a good preacher should be able to wipe out the seven deadly sins. Why do these sins (and others) still exist? I suggest that it is because humans are sinful to the core. These sins are in our essence. As far as I know, no one knows for sure if homosexuality is genetic, socialized, or both. I do believe that there is a genetic component to obesity. Should obese people (and by definition, I am one) be called out the same way that these preachers call out homosexuals? What if homosexuality turns out to be genetic say like eye color or skin color or height or lack of height? Who is responsible for these genetic differences? Is being too short a sin? While the Bible asserts that homosexuality is a sin, I am pretty clear that it is not considered any worse than a long line of sins. None the less, these preachers seem to pound one sin in a hugely disproportional manner: homosexuality.

Are homosexuals bad just because they are homosexuals? Are blondes dumb? Are fat people loathsome? Think about this. In the New Testament, who did Jesus criticize the most? I will let you figure that out but, I guarantee it was not homosexuals.

Should homosexuals have the right to have the same rights as married heterosexual couples? Heck yes, they should. It appalls me that a homosexual couple cannot get their group health benefits to cover the non-employed partner.

Should homosexuals have the right to live their lives without being blatantly discriminated against? Of course they should. It seems awful that an employer might fire some person because he or she is a homosexual. Good grief!

Should homosexuals have the right to get married? Was it Dolly Parton who said, "Gays should suffer like the rest of us." I grew up thinking that the definition of marriage was between a man and a woman or a husband and a wife, which makes it a gender-based relationship. I support and endorse the right of a homosexual couple to have all the rights and responsibilities of a marriage. Call it what you want. I think that it took incredible courage for the President to support gay marriage. Why do I think it took courage? It took courage because I believe that the majority of Americans disagree vehemently with him. How often does a political figure, much less the President of the United States, take an unpopular social position? I think the answer is not very often. You may think it was stupid. You may disagree. I think it took courage.

I really do not think I am homophobic. I really do not. I think the issue is whether one considers homosexual behavior normal. If one does, then I suggest that that person is not a homophobe. I think homosexual behavior is normal (whatever the heck that means). Trust me, I know a lot of people who do not think I am normal.

Welfare

Here we go! This is a hot-button issue for all my Right Winger friends. If homosexuality or feminism is not the end of American society as they see it, then welfare certainly is for sure!

Is welfare some kind of Left Wing conspiracy to undermine Right Wing values and to encourage people to sloth? Do Left Wingers promote welfare to get these welfare people to always vote Democratic because of some kind of welfare bribe? Lots of Righties actually believe this.

Here is something to chew on. "We the people of the United States of America, in order to form a more perfect union, establish justice, insure domestic tranquility, provide for the common defense, **promote the general welfare** and secure the blessings of liberty to ourselves and our general posterity, do ordain and establish this Constitution for the United States of America."

Were the founding fathers of our country Left Wingers? It is obvious that the general welfare was important enough to them to mention it in the Preamble of the Constitution.

I am going to tell everyone a secret. This is fundamental Left Winger philosophy. Whatever is good for the working man or woman is good for America. Notice that I said "working." In my mind, a working person is a person who makes money by one's own direct efforts as opposed to those who make their money by manipulating investments and/or putting deals together. Both can be considered to be work, but I am talking about those among us who go to work versus those among us who invest or deal make. I am not here to disparage deal makers or investors at all. I am just trying to make a distinction for this chapter.

Who would I consider a worker? In my mind, workers would make up the huge majority of the population. I will go on to include retired workers within my definition of workers. Workers include laborers, cooks, plumbers, secretaries, most lawyers, doctors, painters, writers, engineers, architects, druggists, police, firemen, military personnel, teachers, preachers, truck drivers, cowboys, professional athletes, and the list goes on and on. It might be easier to give examples of people who I would not consider to be workers. This would include most upper level executives, real estate developers, wealth managers, investors, board members, business owners, and those who have benefited from inheriting lots of money. I am not sure how to categorize politicians, but they are only a small portion of the population.

Over my lifetime and the lifetimes of my parents, the relationship of a worker to his employer has changed. It seems to me that when I was growing up, a person could earn a living and support his or her spouse and children as a salesperson in a hardware store. Somehow that person could earn enough money to house, feed, and clothe his spouse and kids and these people lived in what I believed was mainstream America. Can that still happen today? Maybe, but it does not seem as likely.

After the Great Depression, the federal government created Social Security. It was a retirement safety net for workers. The government believed that many (some? most?) retired workers would need some supplemental income over and above what they might have saved or earned in a pension from their employer.

I consider Social Security to be one of the greatest legislative initiatives our government ever enacted.

Although Social Security is now underfunded, I do not hear many anti-socialist Right Wingers refusing to accept their Social Security checks when they get old enough to receive them; nor do I hear too much discussion from my Right Winger friends these days telling people how bad Social Security is and how it should be abolished. Republicans may be generally Right Wingers but they are aware that Social Security is here to stay. They may grumble about it, but they do not refuse it. They do not try to get the Republican Party to establish an abolition movement concerning Social Security.

What is Social Security? I believe I would call it welfare. That is right. It is welfare. So all of you Right Wingers who do not want to abolish Social Security should stand out on your front porch right now and yell this: "Balon has just convinced me that I am a huge supporter of welfare." You can continue reading when you come back. If you disagree with me, go out on your front porch and start yelling this, "I want to abolish Social Security." Let's think about it. I doubt any of you took me up on my challenge, but if you yelled you want to abolish Social Security, I disagree, but I admire your convictions.

I am especially interested in how my Right Winger friends talk about Medicare. Once again, they may fuss about it and talk about how our country is going pinko, but when they get old enough, they sign up for it. They want it.

What is Medicare? I would call it welfare. I offer the same hollering challenge for Medicare as I do Social Security.

Now, as we move outward to Medicaid and Aid to Families with Dependent Children (AFDC), the criticism gets louder from my Right Winger friends. These programs are socialism! They are ruining our great country! They are a Left Winger conspiracy to get poor, ignorant people to have more babies so that they can grow up in this welfare state, vote Democrat, ruin our country, and make us Commies! That is essentially the argument.

Is there anyone who really believes that the Left Wingers are spreading around AFDC and Medicare to have more poor babies so that they can grow up to be Democrat shills? If you really believe that, I feel sorry for you. I really do. On this issue you are really off the mark!

Why do we have this Welfare? I believe it is there to create some sort of safety net to help working people when times get tough.

Are there welfare cheats? Are there lazy people who prefer to live at the lowest economic level of poverty and try to beat the system and live a life of sloth? Yes, there are, and I do not know a single person, Left Winger or Right Winger, who has any respect or sympathy for a person like that. Should those people be removed from our welfare rolls? Heck, yes!

Is the welfare cheat problem ruining our country? I doubt it. Is it causing a big waste of money? Sure it is. Should we be more vigilant and diligent in maintaining our welfare rolls? Yes, we should. If people are breaking the law, they should be prosecuted.

Is welfare causing the end of American Society? I do not think so. Is welfare important to the American way of life? Yes, it is.

One must wonder why Right Wingers are against welfare. So many of the Right Wing old and young, family and friends, either depend on it now or plan to when they get older. How can it be so bad?

It does not make sense.

Now, let us think about this issue for a moment. Why would conservative working people be so against welfare when they absolutely plan on accepting it when they get old enough to qualify for it?

If every conservative person was really wealthy, I could understand the logic. I am rich. I will have plenty of money when I get older (or disabled), and I do not need this welfare. Further, I do not want my tax dollars supporting older Americans who have worked their entire lives and contributed to Social Security and Medicare. The irony is that very, very few Americans are rich enough to turn away from these welfare benefits.

Look at a rally of politicians who shout an anti-welfare message. I look at these people on television, and I see working people. I see people who need these benefits. The politician who whips these people into a frenzy certainly benefits from all kinds of government welfare: two big ones are pension benefits and government provided healthcare. Do these politicians shout out, "Take away my government benefits so I can struggle like you?" I have not heard that. Have you heard that?

Why do these politicians say this? Even stranger is why do working people listen to it. Even weirder is why do these working people support politicians who are for cutting the working peoples' welfare while voting to increase the politicians' welfare?

This is an enigma to me.

I want to believe that these working people who support the politicians who claim to want to cut welfare have purity of ideology. I have to take that position, or it will drive me crazier.

So, do you ever hear this statement, "I am a social liberal but a fiscal conservative?" Do you ever utter that statement? This is the group of well meaning but naïve people. To a Left Winger it is like hearing a person say, "I have a lot of black friends." I have never asked anyone to name just one, but I might. What I think when I hear this is "I want my Social Security and Medicare but dang it, I don't want to pay taxes for yours."

I assume that the supporters of the politicians who are for cutting welfare to everyone but themselves think that by reducing benefits their taxes will go down. I guess that is okay, but it certainly seems somewhat self-interested. I want what is mine, but I do not want some of you to have benefits. These people may be thinking that they want their Social Security and their Medicare, but they seem to want to stop aid to families with dependent children.

The logic is that these working people will save income taxes if they get their politicians to vote against welfare. Truthfully, some will save some money on taxes. Most will not because most income taxes are paid by people who make more than the average working person.

The real discussion should be how to more efficiently deliver government services or welfare and to try to see that only those who deserve them should obtain them. It should not be we are becoming communists because we have welfare.

I suggest that if you are a working person who is not rich, you should be arguing for a better plan to support welfare, which you will almost certainly need as you get older and not support those politicians who want to eliminate it.

How hard is that to figure out, really?

The Media

As Ronald Reagan once said, "Here you go again."

And so it is true, here I go again. The enmity which my Right Wingers hold against the media is absurd. I hear it over and over, "The Left Wing media is run by a bunch of you-know-whos in New York City." They believe that these Left Wing media types are subverting our country and promoting their Left Wing, Communist, Socialist, Pinko, Homo, and whatever they can think of agenda.

One listening to this diatribe might think that there was never one, single unflattering story ever written about one Left Winger in the history of our country. For that matter, one might be led to believe that there was never one, single positive story about any Right Winger in the history of our country. You know I am telling the truth!

These Right Wingers think that the media is some sort of evil entity that overwhelms Americans with lies, damn lies, and statistics about every sacred American (Right Wing) institution while promoting the most vile, Left Wing agenda imaginable. When they use the word media, it is usually couched in the expression liberal media!

These Right Wingers make the slightest exception for one particular national television news channel and a number of extreme Right Wing political commentators. However, even these bastions of Right Wing ideology need to watch their "P's and Q's" or other more conservative commentators will condemn them to the throes of the liberal media.

Let's get real. The media is news or story driven. These stories have to be interesting, or people do not follow them (read newspapers, watch TV, listen to the radio, read magazines, or whatever media it is.) If an earthquake occurs, it is a story. I am not aware of political earthquakes. If the Dallas Cowboys beat the Washington Redskins, it is a sports story. There is not much politics to football.

Now, when we talk about political coverage, there is bias all over the place. With the exception of the late, great Walter Cronkite, most news people have some slant. He may have also, but in my mind, he was the greatest. He attended my alma mater, the University of Texas, and had a great voice.

I wish I could say that only right wing politicians blame the media for their problems. Unfortunately, the Left Wingers do, too. I want to say here and now that Left Wingers have never been, nor will they ever be, the whiners that Right Wingers are, but they will whine. It hurts me to mention this, but one of my favorite presidents blamed some kind of Right Wing (media) conspiracy on the coverage (which turned out to be true) of a tryst he had with a particular intern. One would think that all of the coverage on this particular issue was wiped off the face of the media earth. Why do I say this? I say it because no Right Winger will ever acknowledge that the media has ever uttered a bad word about a Democrat.

I can go on and on and on about this or that, but the ultimate truth is that the media is selling stories. There is a Left Wing political agenda, and there is a Right Wing political agenda. If a Left Winger goofs up, you are going to hear about it. If a Right Winger goofs up, you are going to hear about it.

Are there more Left Wing media outlets? Almost certainly there are. Why is that? In my opinion the reason is that a Left Wing slant usually makes more sense than a Right Wing slant. I can hear you Right Wingers screaming! Think about it. This great country operates on a free enterprise system where listeners and advertisers pay to obtain information from the media. If the people or the advertisers wanted more conservative media coverage, the people would get it. People are getting what they want and what they pay for.

Here is an assignment. This will require the ability to use a DVR (digital video recorder). Record the Chris Matthews Show (Hardball) and any Right Wing show. You pick your favorite. Watch them in ten minute segments. Who makes more sense? You decide for yourself. You will feel the slant. I think some of you Lefties actually watch Righty news commentary occasionally. I know I do. You know what I am talking about. You Righties may get converted!

I am also going to whip you guys around a little bit more. The media upholds one of the most treasured rights that we all cherish and share: The right of freedom of speech. The right to criticize our government is sacrosanct. It is one of the pillars of freedom. It is one of the great principles which separate our great nation from one of those communist countries that you Right Wingers hate so much! Get with it; embrace your media!

If you have to watch that Right Wing tripe, do it. Celebrate the First Amendment! Appreciate how fortunate you are to live in a country where we have a free media.

We Left Wingers do.

Patriotism

I am always rankled when I hear my Right Wing friends talk about how patriotic they are and how unpatriotic we Left Wingers are. I looked up patriotism to make sure that I understood what the word meant, and sure enough, I did and do. It is defined as a devoted love, support, and defense of one's country; national loyalty.

Patriotism is a lot like religion. Lots of people claim to have it. Some have it more than others for sure, but a lot of people do not apparently understand what it is.

There are people who think that they are great patriots. There are great patriots, and there are the vast majority of Americans who are certainly patriotic but live their lives without being too concerned about how patriotic they really are.

Why do I get so agitated when I hear my Right Wing buddies brag about how patriotic they are and how unpatriotic the Left Wing is in their opinions? The answer is fairly simple: I believe that Left Wingers are just as patriotic as Right Wingers, if not more so. (I just added that part to stir people up. I really think both sides are equally patriotic.)

The issue usually arises after a bunch of drinking and debating this policy or that policy. If the Right Wingers have not prevailed on the merits of the debate or have been drinking too much, it comes out like this, "If you liberals really loved your country you would understand, but you obviously do not understand because you do not love your country as much as we do."

I know there are Right Wingers who would never think this way but trust me, down in Dallas, Texas, a lot of your political cohorts do. Frankly, I think it is an embarrassingly pathetic way to try to finish an argument, but there it is. So how do we Left Wingers respond to such a banal statement? I guess with characteristic kindness and truthfulness (maybe a little puffing.)

I would say, "Surely you do not believe that in this great land of liberty that just because someone is on the other side of an issue that is important to one and all that an opposing opinion makes that person less patriotic." Now, if that does not even the field of patriotism on a particular issue, I then say that real patriots have sacrificed their lives so that we can have this kind of debate; and to assert that one side of an American debate is less patriotic than another is a slap in the face of the memory of all great patriots who have died to give us the right to debate openly and without fear of governmental reprisal. That works one hundred percent of the time. If it does not work for you, then either you are too drunk to deliver it, or your opponent in the debate is too drunk to listen.

I was at a party not too long ago. A friend of mine was celebrating his sixty-fifth birthday. I could not believe that I have sixty-five-year-old friends but I do! Anyway, he is a former ambassador appointed by President George W. Bush. This was a big party, and I was the only outspoken Left Winger. I praised my friend and related how brilliant he is and how his brilliance had led to many political victories for the Republicans. After

I sat down, another speaker got up and said that the great American Bald Eagle needs two wings to fly, a Right Wing and a Left Wing. I wish I were smart enough to have thought of that.

When you hear certain patriotic songs, does it affect you? It affects me. The first time I heard Whitney Houston sing the National Anthem, I was driving in my car. I was so overwhelmed that I had to pull over to hear it. I was so involved with the beauty and passion she put in the song, I knew I could not drive. Every time I hear her rendition of the National Anthem, I get choked up. I am getting choked up thinking about it now.

America the Beautiful. I tear up every time I sing it and every time I hear it sung by a great singer. In my opinion, Ray Charles "owned it." By that I mean that his version was the absolute best ever, period.

Have you ever read or sung the entire song? I think it is the most inspiring patriotic song ever written. Sing it to yourself.

America the Beautiful

Words by Katharine Lee Bates,
Melody by Samuel Ward

O beautiful for spacious skies,
For amber waves of grain,
For purple mountain majesties
Above the fruited plain!
America! America!
God shed his grace on thee
And crown thy good with brotherhood

From sea to shining sea!

O beautiful for pilgrim feet
Whose stern impassioned stress
A thoroughfare of freedom beat
Across the wilderness!
America! America!
God mend thine every flaw,
Confirm thy soul in self-control,
Thy liberty in law!

O beautiful for heroes proved
In liberating strife.
Who more than self their country loved
And mercy more than life!
America! America!
May God thy gold refine
Till all success be nobleness
And every gain divine!

O beautiful for patriot dream
That sees beyond the years
Thine alabaster cities gleam
Undimmed by human tears!
America! America!
God shed his grace on thee
And crown thy good with brotherhood
From sea to shining sea!

O beautiful for halcyon skies,
For amber waves of grain,
For purple mountain majesties

Above the enameled plain!
America! America!
God shed his grace on thee
Till souls wax fair as earth and air
And music-hearted sea!

O beautiful for pilgrims feet,
Whose stem impassioned stress
A thoroughfare for freedom beat
Across the wilderness!
America! America!
God shed his grace on thee
Till paths be wrought through
wilds of thought
By pilgrim foot and knee!

O beautiful for glory-tale
Of liberating strife
When once and twice,
for man's avail
Men lavished precious life!
America! America!
God shed his grace on thee
Till selfish gain no longer stain
The banner of the free!

O beautiful for patriot dream
That sees beyond the years
Thine alabaster cities gleam
Undimmed by human tears!
America! America!
God shed his grace on thee

> Till nobler men keep once again
> Thy whiter jubilee!

If this song does not bring tears to your eyes, you may need to reconsider your level of patriotism, regardless of your political ideology.

All of us are equally patriotic, Left Winger and Right Winger. Shame on anyone who ever claims his or her side is more patriotic than the other side. Now that you have read this chapter you know the folly of that argument. If you continue to use that argument, the rest of us will think you are an imbecile.

Jobs

When the rest of the world looks at America on television or reads about America in their written media, I think that they all think that we are all rich, and that those of us who work make outlandish salaries, and that our wealth makes many of us decadent. I certainly do not agree that we are a decadent society, but I do believe that we have had the highest standard of living in the world for many years. And you know what? I want to keep it that way.

We have achieved this state of relative prosperity because our middle class workers, both blue and white collar, have been able to make an honest day's pay for an honest day's work. The economic power of our middle class has powered our country. In order for the United States to remain the world power it has been and is, we must protect and support the middle class.

Growing up, it seemed that my friends' parents were able to provide for their families with all kinds of jobs. These people bought homes, cars, raised their families, paid taxes, went on vacations, and shared the optimism that if they worked hard, they would be able to help create a country where their children could be even more financially successful than they were.

This is a belief that everyone I knew seemed to have, Left Winger, Right Winger or No Winger at All.

This Left Winger is not so certain that this sense of optimism is pervasive among working class people any more. That loss of optimism is a terrible thing.

It seems that this great country is in a very precarious situation. While I do care about the debt crisis, I do not think that it is anywhere near the most daunting problem we face as a country concerning our economic future.

The biggest problem, at least in my opinion, is the problem facing a huge percentage of American workers who cannot find jobs that pay a livable wage.

Right Wingers wring their hands about the 50% of the population who do not pay income taxes (they pay plenty of other taxes) and the whatever percentage of the population that receives some type of federal assistance; yet, I think the problem is much deeper and more insidious.

Many American citizen workers do not make enough money to live. It is not so much that these people are underemployed as there are not enough jobs that pay a living wage. That is the real crisis. Something must be done to change this terrible trend in our country.

This is, at least in my mind, a problem that third-world countries have historically faced, not the United States of America! However, what does the future hold?

These third-world countries always seem to have the same economic structure: a small ultra wealthy governing class, the plutocracy, a huge low economic class, and a small and struggling middle class.

This is the direction that I fear our country is headed.

I urge my conservative friends that we do not need to worry about a European form of socialism. We need to worry about a Central and South American form of plutocracy!

The average working American worker's earnings have scantly increased in adjusted dollars in the last thirty years while corporate executive compensation has increased greatly, which, of course, creates a greater and greater gap between the wealthy and the working class. This is not right.

What has happened in the course of history when the wealth of countries has concentrated into a smaller and smaller percentage of the population while poverty increases? Everyone knows what happens: political unrest, misery, destabilized economies, loss of hope for the existing structure of government, and anger and frustration at the aristocratic social organization.

What will happen if over time enough Americans get to the point where they cannot support themselves? If middle class hope in our economic future fails, what will the workers in this country do? They will do what the workers and the oppressed would do in any country. They will revolt. I mean violently, just like our south of the border friends.

This is not a problem that I believe is imminent. It is not a problem that I believe is unfixable, but it is a big problem. If we sit by idly, it will get worse. We need a vision to reinvigorate the American Dream. This is what everyone should want, and I mean everyone.

Is there one easy, simple answer, like always vote for the most liberal candidate? Even though that is generally a very good strategy, the answer is probably not. We all need to pull together to improve the working wage of our working people.

If we do not figure out a strategy, I see our country going into decline. We will lose our status as the greatest country in the world. This is not a problem that any one group or any one state can solve. It is too big. It is going to take the collective efforts of the best minds we have working together and not sniping and bickering.

There may be some of my Right friends who sincerely believe that capitalism is almost omniscient in its greatness and fairness and by merely saying the word free enterprise, all our economic and social woes will disappear.

I absolutely do not believe that unregulated private enterprise will solve this issue. In fact, I believe that unregulated private enterprise is the *biggest culprit* to this emerging problem.

I believe that many of our business leaders have lost their way. Instead of trying to operate a business that provides the best products or services and providing adequate wages and benefits for its employees, they have become seduced by the short-term bottom line.

Many manufacturing companies moved their jobs overseas and pay their employees abroad very, very low wages, and they do not have to provide any benefits. What is the short-term result of this short sighted decision: profits!

What are the long-term consequences of this type of thinking? Think about it? Sending more and more good paying American jobs to this or that third-world country can do nothing but reduce the opportunity in the United States for middle class people to have good jobs and support their families.

Let us say you are the type of business leader who does not give a pickle about American workers. For this diatribe, let's say you manufacture televisions. You send all of the manufacturing and supervisory jobs in your company to wherever. Your stock soars. Your Board of Directors praises you. You get a big raise. You get all kinds of benefits. You are the example of brilliant American business leadership. What happens next? Your competitors start to follow suit. They send all their jobs over to a different country. They follow your paradigm. Since they had a little more opportunity to do research where they could pay their employees less and provide less safety protection for their employees, they can sell their products cheaper than you. Now they are in the spotlight. Their company stock soars. Their Boards of Directors praise them as being even more brilliant than you! They get bigger raises. They get better benefits. Hooray for free enterprise! Our top executives have figured how to get rich and how to improve the value of their stock. Now everyone is doing this. American workers are let go. Good jobs go to third-world countries where the workers will work for much less money, and the working conditions are much worse. Unfortunately, some Americans actually think this is good.

Who loses out? Initially, it is the American workers and their families. They lose their good jobs to some foreigner in a foreign country. Sure, they had stock in their former company, which has dramatically increased in value, but they had to sell it to have enough money to keep their homes from foreclosure and to support their families. These are hard working Americans. They go out and find jobs. Unfortunately, they cannot obtain a job that pays as much as their last job did, because that job is no longer in the United States. If they are lucky, they can sell their house and buy a cheaper one. If not, then they lose it. This becomes a huge problem.

For some time, the politicians and business leaders beat their chests and tell anyone who will listen what geniuses they are and what a great job they are doing to protect the American free enterprise system. People who have not lost their jobs still listen. This exportation of jobs still sounds great. Their stock is rising. Their wealth is growing. They ignore the for sale signs in their neighborhoods. They say "good bye" to their friends who have to move. They must think it will all work out as it always has. Heck, those are the breaks. That is free enterprise!

Time passes, and some of these people who so heartily supported job exportation begin to lose their jobs. Now they must sell their homes. They must find any job they can to survive. They have to sell their stock. They now wonder what happened.

More time passes. More American workers lose their jobs. Fewer and fewer can afford the things that they could afford in the past. The buying power of the entire middle class begins to shrink. They spend less money because they have less money.

Guess what happens next? The entire industry disappears from America. They get bought by foreign companies, or they just close down. We no longer manufacture televisions in America. All these people that participated in the manufacturing of televisions in America have lost their jobs.

Eventually, our economy shrinks. The American middle class shrinks. Some politicians and business leaders will say this is the inevitability of the global economy. I say it is the consequence of greed and self interest on the part of many of our business leaders and their puppet politicians both Republican and Democrat.

I know that you Left Wingers are shouting "Amen" and you Right Wingers are saying "what a bunch of hog wash!" I hope that my philosophy prevails so you can keep your hog to wash.

Left Wingers are for working-class people. Who are the working-class people? Almost all of us are or were working class people. It is not so important in my definition whether one is a laborer, a banker, a lawyer, a doctor, a teacher, a small business owner or what, as long as one works for his or her living. That is my definition of a working-class person. By the way, a retired working-class person is a working-class person as far as I am concerned. There are working- class people who make a whole lot of money and there are a lot of working-class people who are unemployed yet are still working-class people. Working-class people should fall somewhere in what most people think of as the middle class.

If these American people cannot obtain and maintain a job that pays a wage great enough to provide for basic necessities without some form of governmental aid, then we have a serious problem. Surely, no one disagrees.

What does a person need to earn to provide for his or her family? I guess it varies from person to person and place to place, but think of what it costs for basics. It would be hard to provide for a family of four at $15.00 per hour. That is about $30,000 per year. Do some research. How many companies pay their workers hourly or salaried positions of $30,000? Do a little more research. Look at the compensation rate for the highest paid executives in these companies. What do they make? Do they make 30 times what the average worker makes? That would be $900,000. Is it possible that these executives make 100 times more than the average worker makes? That is $3,000,000. What if these executives make 200 times what the average worker makes? This would be $6,000,000. Check out some of your favorite companies and see what is published.

This Left Winger is not really griping at the amount of money paid to the executives of these companies, he is griping about how little is paid to the employees of these companies!

We need to do some serious soul searching. We need to figure out how to create more and better paying jobs for Americans!

The logic screams to me that we overpay many executives while we underpay the working class.

I cannot make anyone do anything. I can make suggestions.

Do shareholders really have the power to pressure the Boards of Directors to require the upper executives to adjust the distribution of the compensation structure in a corporation? It is possible, but what a difficult task.

Can shareholders force their Boards to force their executives to keep American jobs in America? It will be hard, but if we work together, we can, and we can be profitable.

I am going to really preach the gospel of the Left Winger. In this Lefty's opinion, this should be our mantra: Buy American. Let me say it again, **Buy American.**

We need to buy American when we can. We need to create an environment where the American heavy industry can resurrect itself. We need to STOP exporting many of our best jobs overseas. We need a tax code that treats the wealthy and the middle class the same. There are zillions of good ideas abounding. We need to sort through them and work together to find good American solutions. Buy American!

I have to tell you an anecdote about a discussion I was having with a Right Wing friend of mine (whose name will remain anonymous because I am still trying to convert him). He was deriding all liberals and especially President Obama, calling all of us socialists. He went on to say that socialism is a terrible form of oppression, and that socialist countries cannot produce any products that can compare to good old American capitalist products. I believe that he thinks that anyone who thinks rich people should pay the same percentage of income taxation as the working class is a socialist. Using that definition, almost everyone except some Republicans are socialists. I simply asked why he drives a BMW. That discussion ended quickly. Unfortunately, I cannot solve the problem of low-paying jobs in America that easily, but you can. **Buy American!**

Both parties had better come to recognize this problem, or we will insidiously become a third-world country. Trust me, there is plenty of blame to go around. Left Wingers, Right Wingers, everyone has let this happen. So you do your part. **Buy American!**

Having watched our Congress bicker over the 2011 debt ceiling, I was extremely discouraged. It was appalling to me that the leaders in both parties had to tell the rank and file Congressmen to act like adults. The incivility and lack of effort to work on a satisfactory compromise was a very ugly scar on our elected officials. If we are to be successful in creating more and better jobs in this country, we will need more civility, more cooperation, more creative thinking, and more sacrifice. We need to **Buy American!**

It is a real problem that jobs do not pay enough money for American workers to live. You can help. **Buy American!**

Okay, you are a cynic. You do not believe that American products are good enough for you. American products are not a good enough value for you. If you feel that way, let us join together and demand the highest quality products from American manufacturers. Do you believe that the American laborer is lazy? If that is so, why do foreign automobile manufacturers build cars in the United States? They do because these foreign manufacturers know Americans are great workers.

How many of you own a vehicle? How many of you own an American vehicle? Do you own foreign vehicles because you are not a patriot? I doubt it. You own a foreign vehicle because you believe that the foreign vehicle is a better vehicle or a better value for you. I guess if you drive a Lamborghini you do not fit this paradigm I am discussing.

Anyway, trust me, American cars are getting better. Are they universally rated the best in the world yet? No, they are not. Can they become the best? Yes, they can. We must just commit to that idea and then make it happen. Will it happen over night? Of course not. You can make it happen faster if you will **Buy American!**

I earnestly believe this. We can and must work together. We must speak with our pocket books. Let us look for American products. Let us praise American manufacturers who make world-class goods and provide world-class service.

If you still think that American labor is not the best in the World, why do we have the absolute best military weaponry? Do we buy it from the Chinese? No, we buy it from American manufacturers who hire American labor. You all know this is right.

If you are a whiner who believes that unions have ruined American manufacturing, I will write a book that I hope will correct your thinking. Just remember this. American labor union membership is the hardest working group of people in the world. They always have been and, hopefully, they will have the opportunity to keep on in the future. Who builds our submarines? Who builds our aircraft carriers? Who builds our aircraft both civilian and military? When the American automotive industry dominated the world, who built those cars? The answer is clear. American union workers did. God Bless them and God Bless America. Seriously, can anyone actually believe that unions are bad for America? If they are good for the American worker, then they are good for America.

If "We the People" do not stand up for American workers, eventually they will stand up against those who have oppressed them and deservedly so. **Buy American!**

Immigration

To many, this is another volatile issue. While I am not certain this is a Left-Right issue, this is my Left Winger solution.

First, it is silly to think we can round up all the illegal aliens, deport them, and then keep them out of the country. Even if we just concentrated on illegal aliens from Mexico, the cost, time, and effort would be ridiculous. The lawsuits from the wrongful deportation of Hispanic-American citizens would make border state lawyers rich. (I think lots of Right Wingers would rather have illegal aliens than rich lawyers). So when you hear your favorite politician yakking about how he or she would deport all the illegal aliens in this country, remember this is either a flat out lie, or this politician is too dumb to hold office. That means if that politician is already in office, you should vote against him or her at your earliest opportunity.

I certainly agree that we need to be able to control the access of those entering our country. No Left Winger in the world wants terrorists to enter the United States, legally or illegally.

What are the real reasons that people want to get rid of these illegal aliens? Two reasons, at least in my mind: economics and racism. I have no solution for racism, but I have an idea or two about economics.

Many believe that the illegal alien is a burden to society because they do not pay their fair share of taxes, and they use our governmental benefits at a disproportionate rate compared to legal aliens and citizens. Let us assume that this is true, whether it is or not. When I use the word "taxes," I am referring to income taxes. Illegal immigrants do pay sales taxes and property taxes.

There are some who believe that illegal aliens take jobs from Americans because they will work for a lower rate than an American would for the same job. It does seem to me that in our history, immigrants have always entered the country at the low end of the economic chain and then worked their way up. So, I agree that the illegal aliens do take a lot of low paying labor intensive jobs.

How do we handle the problem? I believe the most logical answer is to make available work permits for all aliens who apply who do not have a serious criminal record (say a felony). There should be legitimate background checks here and in the home countries of these applicants. The fee for obtaining one should be minimal. I would not require any applicant to go back to his or her home country. That is absurd, unnecessary, and wasteful.

After an applicant is qualified, he or she will be issued a high tech work permit card. These cards must be secured, not easily counterfeited, and be able to go through some type of scanning for verification purposes.

I know that many of my Left Wing friends will disagree about the work permits as some sort of national identity card. Frankly, I would expect some of my Righty friends to oppose this idea on those grounds, also. That is one of the great things about being a Left Winger; you do not have to follow in lock step with other liberal thinking people. (Maybe even a few Right Wingers think that, too.) Anyway, I think it is a good idea, and that is why I am telling you.

All aliens must have and present the work permit card to his or her employer. All work permit workers will be deemed to be employees of their employer. The fiction of the subcontractor will not apply to these people. This means that their employers will be responsible for these workers' negligence when it occurs. If the employer provides benefits for any of these alien employees, then it must provide benefits for all.

The employer must also withhold what I would describe as an employment tariff for the wages these alien workers would make. The tariff will increase as the alien stays in the United States without becoming a lawful citizen. There would be no special deductions for the employer. The tariff would be accounted as salary paid to the employer.

For example, for the first five years, an alien's work tariff would be 15% of his or her gross wages. The next five years, the work tariff would increase to 20% of his or her gross wages and the next five years the work tariff would increase to 25% and then max out at 30%.

This money would be evenly split between the Local, State and the Federal Government.

What would be the penalties for violations of this law?

Any alien worker working without a work permit would be deported. It would be a felony for that individual to return to the United States. Why would I make this such a serious offense? I would because it would be so easy to obtain the work permit. Anyone who flaunts the law would be punished. There are lots of people who would cherish the opportunity to legally come to the United States of America and work.

Any employer who employs alien workers in violation of this law would receive incarceration and a fine. Both the fine and incarceration would increase for subsequent violations.

I would recommend that for a first violation, the employer would serve seven days in jail and pay a $1,000 fine. A second violation would be thirty days in jail and a $5,000 fine. Any subsequent violations would require a six-month sentence and a $10,000 fine. Absolutely no probation would be allowed.

You may be thinking how could a liberal cream puff want to incarcerate any employer for this type of non-violent violation of the law? Well, I strongly believe in fairness and rules. This law, if implemented the way I envision, would be so easy to follow that a violation should be enforced and there must be enough teeth in the sentence to actually deter an employer from cheating or breaking the law. Heck, my Right Wing friends might like this more than my Left Wing friends just because of the penal aspect.

The associated border security issue must also be addressed. As for unauthorized border crossings, we would use our best technology to stop any illegal entries into the country. The use of deadly force could be authorized if appropriate, which means for international drug dealers and terrorist types and not a kid who is fishing in Falcon Lake and motors over to our side. This may seem draconian, but it would be so easy to lawfully travel into the USA that there would be no need for anyone to try to enter illegally unless he or she had illegal intentions such as drug importation or terrorism. Naturally, we would still extend visitation visas for those aliens who want to come to the USA and spend their money on a vacation and then return home without trying to secure work.

I am not a techie and I do not think political ideology really is important to the technological geniuses who will invent the gear we will need to implement this strategy.

I would also make it easier to become an American citizen. It is an extremely hard, long, and expensive process to do so now. What do I think should be the requirements of American citizenship? First, I think that all naturalized Americans must be able to speak, read, and write English. They do not need to be as fluent as James Earl Jones, but it is essential to be successful in this country to have a working understanding of the English Language. I know that English is not the official language of the USA, but come on; it is the language that all Americans use to speak, transact business, and enact laws.

The second requirement would be for all naturalized citizens to pass a civics class. For that matter, I wish it were required for every American to do this. All Americans should have a passable understanding of our history and culture. It is shocking to me how many native-born Americans do not possess this knowledge.

The third requirement would be that during the pre-citizenship residency period where the applicant alien is learning English and civics, which I think should be five years, the applicant must be free from felony or moral turpitude criminal convictions.

Naturally, once an alien has fulfilled these requirements,he or she would now have all the rights and responsibilities of natural citizens including the right to pay income taxes! My tariff would no longer apply to the new citizen.

I want to reemphasize that this should not be an expensive process.

I would hope that between my tariff concept and the easier requirements to becoming a naturalized American, more immigrants would be encouraged to acculturate into our economic and social society.

Is this really a Left-Right issue? I am not even sure. So, if you agree that this is a good idea you could still be a Right Winger in good standing.

The Good Old Days

I hear people lamenting how everything seems to have gone to hell in a hand basket. I love that phrase. It usually means that things sure were better in the good old days.

I even hear that religion has suffered and that we should long for the good old days when I suppose they believe everyone lived a high moral and Christian life.

Do you remember the TV show, *All in the Family*? I loved it. I especially loved the introductory song. It was written by Lee Adams (lyrics) and Charles Strouse (music). Carroll O'Connor and Jean Stapleton sang the song, and it was awesome. Why don't you sing it right now?

> **"Those Were The Days"**
> by Lee Adams and Charles Strouse

> Boy, the way Glen Miller played. Songs that made the hit parade.

> Guys like us, we had it made. Those were the days.

> Didn't need no welfare state. Everybody pulled his weight.

> Gee, our old LaSalle ran great. Those were the days.

And you know who you were then, girls were girls and
men were men.

Mister, we could use a man like Herbert Hoover again.

People seemed to be content. Fifty dollars paid the rent.

Freaks were in a circus tent. Those were the days.

Take a little Sunday spin, go to watch the Dodgers win.

Have yourself a dandy day that cost you under a fin.

Hair was short and skirts were long. Kate Smith really
sold a song.

I don't know just what went wrong. Those Were The
Days.

I hope you have heard this song because it is so great. It is a
satire.

What is it about people who think that things were better in
the good old days? Is it possible that there are Left Wingers
who lament the good old days? Maybe I am so indoctrinated
with Left Wing ideology that I think it is only Right Wingers
who pine for a return of the good old days.

I am a believer that we are currently living in the good days.
I believe that these days are the best days. Gosh, when would
anyone think days were better than they are now? Even in
Texas, where we are overwhelmed by Right Wingers, these are
the good old days. Of course, when Texans finally wake up
and start electing Left Wingers to state wide offices, then those
days will even be better days!

Were the early 1800's the good old days here in America? We
had the United States Constitution and the Bill of Rights. We

did not have an income tax. However, if one happened to be a Native American or a slave, maybe it was not such a good era. By the way, were women allowed to vote?

We did have to fight the Civil War. I do not see how anyone could believe that those were the good old days.

Let us look forward to the late 1800's. Still no income tax! Slavery had been abolished, but no human being on the planet could argue that freed slaves or Native Americans were sharing an equal portion of the American Way. Surely, women could vote? Not!

I have not even mentioned technology. I am just talking about the law and the way people interacted with each other.

Now let us look toward the early 1900s. Oops, we now have the income tax. Jim Crow laws are rampant. Working people of all races and creeds are not unionized. The wealthy are getting wealthier at the expense of the poor. The Native Americans are still being mistreated.

Do I have to keep going on and on? Maybe I do. In the early 1900's, we had a worldwide influenza epidemic, which ravaged the population. What about World War One? Were these the good old days?

Do you remember what happened August 18, 1920? The Nineteenth Amendment was ratified. Now, women have the right to vote! Now that was a good day!

In the 1930's and 1940's, what about the rise of Nazism? The Depression? The Dust Bowl? The Holocaust? The growth of Communism? World War Two? Were those the good old days?

The Fabulous Fifties! I was born in the Fabulous Fifties! Were they the good old days? Maybe for some they were. We had labor unions. We had Elvis! We had Mickey Mantle and Willie Mays. Las Vegas was growing. The Mob was getting more powerful. We had the Poll Tax, segregation, the Ku Klux Klan, and we had the constant threat of nuclear warfare (or at least that is what we were told). Did women really have equal rights in the workplace? (short answer: no). I will admit, I liked the 1950's, especially the Rock and Roll and Major League Baseball, which was now integrated.

The Sixties, my formative years; were they the good old days? We made some progress for sure. We had the Civil Rights Act. We had the beginning of real desegregation. We had the Beatles! We had race riots. We had the Viet Nam Conflict (War). We had student demonstrations. We had the proliferation of drugs. We began white flight from integrated neighborhoods.

This is boring me so it must really be boring for you. Where are we now? We have had a technological explosion. In the United States of America, who does not have a good color TV? Who does not have a cell phone or a computer or access to the internet. Our schools are better. We have better opportunities for all people. The United States is a darn good place to live right now. Is it perfect? No, it is not, but it is getting better. These are the good old days.

Maybe if Carroll O'Connor were still with us he would sing, "These are the days!"

The Future and Making it Work Better

I wrote this book to emphasize that we are all Americans, first and foremost. We are not the enemy. Left Wingers and Right Wingers share a common political system, culture, and basic value system. We need to understand each other better.

We have to quit demonizing each other. Trust me, I know Left Wingers demonize Right Wingers as much as the Right Wingers demonize Left Wingers.

I am urging all of us to put a stop to that polarizing, counterproductive, and idiotic behavior. If your political representatives are demonizing politicians on the other side of an issue, call him or her out on it. Let that person and everyone within ear shot know that we have to work together. That type of politics is yesterday's politics in what was once believed by many as the good old days. It was bad politics then. It is bad politics today. If it continues it will continue to be bad politics tomorrow.

If there is anything to be learned from this book, it is Left Wingers and Right Wingers both believe that we are a great nation. We share a great history. It has not always been smooth or pretty. Frankly, much of it has been outright awful, but we continued to persevere. If we work together, Left and Right, we will continue to be the greatest nation the world has ever known. We can do it. We should do it, and we must do it. We owe that commitment to the legacy of our Founding Fathers. We owe that commitment to the great patriots who gave all they had on the field of battle to ensure and preserve our rights and freedoms. We owe that commitment to ourselves. We owe that commitment to our children and grandchildren. It has long been a tradition in this great country that the older generation would pave the way for the next generation to have better lives.

The most important ideas I have to share are that we should work together, that we must do everything we can to preserve the middle class and that we should **Buy American**!

Let the great traditions of our Great Country continue.

God Bless America and God Bless you.

Epilogue

I do want to thank you for reading my first literary effort. I have learned that books do not write themselves, and it took me forever to finish this one.

The presidential election of 2012 is now history. Thank goodness it is! Even though I love politics, the campaigns wore me out.

I have no idea how any human being could bear up to the rigors of a presidential campaign.

I am amazed that the candidates can do it. I admire them. I praise them; all of them. They make huge sacrifices to run for the highest offices in the land, and they should be lauded. It makes me bristle when otherwise well meaning people dismiss their efforts as anything other than patriotic and dutiful acts.

President Obama won. I believe that the final numbers were 50.6% of Americans voting for President Obama and 47.8 % of Americans voting for Governor Romney. That seems pretty close to me and nowhere near a landslide. However, it does seem that the Republicans are acting as if it were.

I also thank the 121,745,725 Americans who cast their votes. Shame on those of you who did not.

Why did President Obama get re-elected? I think because he and the Democrats proposed a platform which was more favorable to the working middle class than Mitt Romney and the Republicans. That is that, period.

Do I think that President Obama was vulnerable? Yes I do. There are lots of reasons that he was vulnerable but the biggest weakness, at least in my mind, was the high rate of joblessness in America.

Did the Republicans exploit that weakness to their best advantage? Who knows? I think that it is amazing that the Republicans did as well as they did. I do not believe that they lost because Mitt Romney ran a bad campaign. I think that they lost because what the Republican party thinks is conservative ideology is badly out of step with the middle class, the emerging minority voters, and women.

In the aftermath of the election loss, there is a bunch of finger pointing within the Republican party. I suppose that is always the case when you lose. I thought that Al Gore lost because he did not effectively use Bill Clinton to campaign for him. I may be wrong, but that is what I thought.

I do not believe that there is one issue or platform that cost the Republicans the election. I am quite certain that some of the reasoning for the loss that is being put forth by some of the Right Wing pundits is absolutely absurd.

What do I think is so absurd? Here are a few examples.

We lost because of Hurricane Sandy. Really? Do they believe that God actually intervened to create a hurricane to ensure a Democratic victory? That is hilarious to me. Maybe they have completely given up on the Lord. I doubt it, but who knows.

We lost because the Democrats promised stuff to all those people who do not do anything but take from the government. This is the kind of reasoning that will make the Republican party a footnote in history. The only thing I remember is that the Republicans promised to give tax breaks to people, and that under no circumstance would the Republicans do anything to raise the taxes on the richest Americans so that they would pay the same percentage as the upper middle working class does. Now that is some promised stuff.

We lost because of the Mexicans. I guess they mean Americans with Hispanic heritage. Democrats know that not everyone with a Hispanic surname hails from Mexico. Do they think that these people should not be allowed to vote? They lost all the minority vote because the minorities, like other working class Americans, know that the Republican platform favors the wealthy over them. Good grief, does it take John Maynard Keynes to figure that out? My suggestion would be to start out by not taking such an anti-immigration stance and work from there. My legal assistant, Isabell Sanchez, told me that she could imagine how much criticism a Hispanic Democratic Presidential candidate would receive over the birth certificate issue. She said that she could hear it now, "That Hispanic candidate was born in Mexico, not the United States."

We lost because America has lost its work ethic, and a real American just does not have a chance anymore against a socialist. That is such an ignorant opinion that it is almost too stupid to even address, but I will, of course. First, it presupposes that only real Americans vote Republican. That is so offensive it makes not only my face turn red but must anger all of our Left Winger servicemen and women who have fought and continue to fight for our great country. Anyone who believes that should feel shame. Second, it ignorantly assumes that Americans are lazy slobs. If that were so, why do Honda, Toyota, Nissan, Subaru, Mazda, Mitsubishi, BMW, Mercedes Benz, and Volkswagen build vehicles in the United States? These foreign manufacturers build their vehicles here because they know that the hardest working and best labor in the world is right here in the United States of America. Calling the other side socialist? Now that is another ignoramus position. Democrats disagree with us so they must be socialists. Give it up. If you really feel that way, please give up your Social Security and Medicare. Better yet, organize a demonstration to protest to your Republican Senators and Representatives about not fighting hard enough to repeal those two programs. That is pathetic.

The Republicans lost because they have lost their way. I am a two-party system guy. I do not want the Republican party to disappear. I want it to reassess itself. Democrats are not the enemy. We are all Americans. We need to work together.

If after reading this book, I have not convinced any of you Right Wingers that you are really Left Wingers, that is okay. Hopefully, you will at least believe that we are not that different.

Instead of whining like crazy, take a look in the mirror. Think about it.

I am only going to say this once more: **Buy American!**

The Author

Balon Buchanan Bradley was born in 1953 in Pine Bluff, Arkansas. His father was serving in the Army at the time.

His father, Gene Buchanan "Buck" Bradley had a Ph. D. in Chemistry and was a partner in Quality Chemical Company in Austin, Texas. Buck Bradley was killed in an explosion at the chemical company in 1960.

That was the most important point of the author's life. It changed his course.

His mother, Betty Ann Biel Bradley Edgerton went back to the University of Texas and obtained her Masters Degree and Ph. D. in Science Education.

His mother moved Balon and his younger brother, Blake, with her to Abilene, Texas, where she accepted a teaching position at McMurry College.

The greatest mentor, liberal, parent, and person in his life was his mother, which of course, made him a "momma's boy." This is a moniker he has lovingly embraced his entire life.

Betty Ann left a huge footprint on those who knew her. Her goal was for him to achieve a doctorate degree and become a missionary before he was twenty-five. He managed the doctorate degree but did not hear the call of mission work.

Balon graduated from Oscar Henry Cooper High, The University of Texas, and the University of Houston Law School.

After graduating from law School, Balon went to work for the Dallas County District Attorney. After three years as an assistant district attorney, he left to start his private practice.

Balon has a personal injury practice in Dallas.

Balon is married to Anne and has two wonderful children, Alison and Katharine.

Balon is a liberal. He wants you to understand what liberals think. He believes that liberals and conservatives share a majority of core values and great love of the United States.

53257600R00098

Made in the USA
Columbia, SC
16 March 2019